~ Mixed-Media ~
COLLAGE JEWELRY

~ Mixed-Media ~
COLLAGE JEWELRY

New Directions in Memory Jewelry

Janette Schuster

LARK BOOKS

A Division of Sterling Publishing Co., Inc.
New York / London

EDITOR: Brian Sawyer

MANAGING EDITORS: Aimee Chase and
Rebecca Springer

COPYEDITOR: Genevieve d'Entremont

ART DIRECTOR: Wendy Simard

INTERIOR DESIGNER: Laura McFadden Design /
Clicked Creative

COVER DESIGNER: Cindy LaBreacht

ASSISTANT ART DIRECTOR: Seth Dolinsky

EDITORIAL ASSISTANCE: Eric Grzymkowski

PHOTOGRAPHER: Allan Penn

PHOTOGRAPHY MANAGER: David Urbina

PROOFREADER: Kathy Dragolich

*To my best friend and sister,
Beth, who is always on my side.*

A Lark/Hollan Book
Produced by Hollan Publishing, Inc.
100 Cummings Center, Suite 125G, Beverly, MA 01915

Library of Congress Cataloging-in-Publication Data

Schuster, Janette, 1960-
   Mixed-media collage jewelry : new directions in memory jewelry /
Janette Schuster. -- 1st ed.
      p. cm.
   Includes bibliographical references and index.
   ISBN-13: 978-1-60059-268-3 (hc-plc with jacket : alk. paper)
   ISBN-10: 1-60059-268-6 (hc-plc with jacket : alk. paper)
1. Jewelry making. 2. Collage. I. Title.
   TT212.S376 2009
   739.27--dc22
                                          2008001513

10 9 8 7 6 5 4 3 2 1

First Edition

Published by Lark Books, A Division of Sterling Publishing Co., Inc.
387 Park Avenue South, New York, NY 10016

HOLLAN   © 2008 by Hollan Publishing, Inc.

Distributed in Canada by Sterling Publishing
c/o Canadian Manda Group, 165 Dufferin Street
Toronto, Ontario, Canada M6K 3H6
Distributed in the United Kingdom by GMC Distribution Services
Castle Place, 166 High Street, Lewes, East Sussex, England BN7 1XU
Distributed in Australia by Capricorn Link (Australia) Pty. Ltd.
P.O. Box 704, Windsor, NSW 2756, Australia

Manufactured in China

ISBN-13: 978-1-60059-268-3
ISBN-10: 1-60059-268-6

For information about custom editions, special sales, premium
and corporate purchases, please contact Sterling Special Sales
Department at 800-805-5489 or specialsales@sterlingpublishing.com.

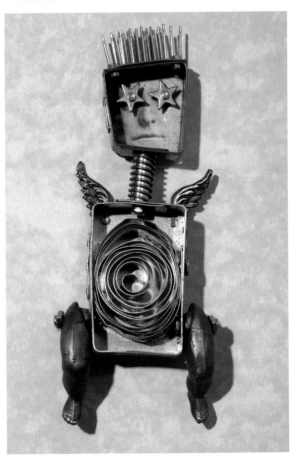

contents

introduction

OUR MEMORIES ARE WHAT keep the past alive for us. They keep our personal histories a part of our present lives. When the artifacts of our personal histories are used to create collage jewelry, that jewelry becomes a highly personal treasure, as unique as a thumbprint.

Collage Jewelry and Its Roots

If you are not already familiar with the art form of collage, you might think of a collage as the artistic equivalent of a good party, in which disparate elements are brought together to form a balanced and pleasing whole. In a collage, a collection of unrelated things (such as photos, newspaper, cloth, and found objects) is adhered or joined together for creative expression. When this diverse assemblage of materials becomes sculptural adornment, you have collage jewelry.

Collage jewelry is not, as you might assume, solely a contemporary art form spawned in the twentieth or twenty-first century. In a sense, people have always made collage jewelry, since they have always fitted together whatever was available to them—materials either found or traded—to adorn themselves. Every early jewelry maker was a collage or found object artist. Some of the earliest collage jewelry materials included products of nature such as flowers, amber, and fossils, and animal parts such as feathers, teeth, bones, claws, shells, and horn. Early people made or wore such adornments for a variety of very personal reasons: to show wealth or social status, for religious expression, for protection from disease or evil, to promote luck, to present as a gift, and for ornamentation. They even made jewelry to

> "When the artifacts of our personal histories are used to create collage jewelry, that jewelry becomes a highly personal treasure, as unique as a thumbprint."

celebrate their heritage or past, much like many of the modern jewelry artists whose work appears in this book.

In medieval and Victorian times, people wore *chatelaines*: waist ornaments consisting of utilitarian objects such as keys, scissors, writing tablets, watches, and seals suspended from chains. The sentimental Victorians used jewelry to express their passions and as mementos of loved ones, whether living or dead. Their lockets and brooches often encased photographs and locks of hair. And, as avid naturalists, they even used real insects and bird heads in jewelry. Ever the incurable romantic, Queen Victoria wore a bracelet made with her children's baby teeth and mourning jewelry in memory of her much-loved husband, Albert. Even Victorian men wore a collage of connected chains, watches, seals, compasses, and fobs hanging from their vests.

LEFT: Jewelry made of shell, bone, and horn

In the 1930s to 1950s, a modernist jewelry movement, which included the works of surrealist-inspired jeweler Sam Kramer, brought found objects like meteorites, shells, and glass taxidermy eyes to collage jewelry. In the 1960s and 1970s, jewelry innovators such as Fred Woell, Robert Ebendorf, and Thomas Mann laid the foundation for today's collage jewelry, incorporating materials such as ephemera, photos, polystyrene foam, and acrylic in their jewelry. All three artists carry on and expand the tradition today, continuing to create collage jewelry with unique materials and teaching their techniques to twenty-first-century artists (see the instructions for Thomas Mann's Found Object Sandwich Pin on page 127).

How to Use This Book

The making of a piece of collage jewelry can be a very personal journey when its ingredients include the maker's keepsakes and mementos. *Mixed-Media Collage Jewelry* was written to help you take that journey by both instructing and inspiring you. It shows examples of creative, sophisticated, and artistic collage jewelry made with vintage and new materials such as buttons, photos, family

mementos, and found objects. These one-of-a-kind pieces celebrate and commemorate the life events, relationships, and passions of their makers.

In this book you will find twenty-five how-to projects designed by myself and eleven other artists. The projects range in skill level from beginning to advanced. If you are new to jewelry making, I suggest you first familiarize yourself with the tools and materials in the first section and try a few of the basic techniques described in the second section. Just using the basic skills of cutting, sawing, drilling, and riveting, you can make impressive collage jewelry. Then, try a simple project like the Domino Necklace on page 32. Don't be intimidated by a technique or project that seems challenging. As a beginner, remember that each jewelry artist represented in this book was once in your shoes, too.

If you have already mastered jewelry-making techniques, use the projects in this book as inspiration—for new materials to use and ways to pull them together in your own very personal memory jewelry. Let the more advanced projects in the last chapter provide fresh inspiration worthy of a master-class experience in jewelry making. Before you know it, you'll be making amazing jewelry like Kristin Diener's Leaving Home Necklace on page 134.

Regardless of your skill level, keep in mind that you don't need exactly the same kinds of mementos used by a particular artist for a given project; you can start making similar collage jewelry using your own materials. Think of each project merely as a starting point. As you read the instructions and look at the illustrations, ask yourself: What materials and mementos do I have right now that I can use? How can I apply these techniques to make my own unique piece, using the keepsakes I have on hand?

A Word About Art, Fear, and Being Original

I'll never forget my first trip to Europe. If I had listened to my fears and those of my mother, I never would have crossed the Atlantic. I wouldn't have seen the view from the top of the Eiffel Tower, walked the same lanes Jane Austen did, or scanned Loch Ness for its monster. I wouldn't be the same person or artist I am today.

All the artists in this book experienced trepidation when they took a new path or tested new skills. I invite you to stretch your jewelry-making skills today by trying something in this book that might seem a bit intimidating. Keep trying things that are more challenging, and you will be surprised by what you can create.

We all learn by mimicry, by watching others and trying exactly what they do. It's a good way to start. But I challenge you to go a step further and add your own twist to each project in this book. Before you know it, you won't just be approximating someone else's art—you will be "singing with your own voice," or making collage jewelry from the heart and imbued with your own life story. You can do it. I believe in you. Now go forth, preserve a few memories, and make collage jewelry.

tools and materials

THE RIGHT TOOLS really do make jewelry tasks easier. And without materials, there can be no jewelry. This chapter provides a general overview of many tools and materials you'll need for the techniques and projects in the upcoming chapters. In the introductions to the project chapters, you'll find further discussions of materials specific to the jewelry in those chapters.

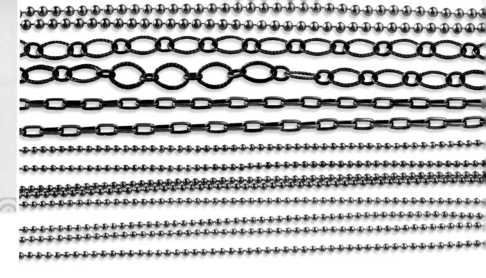

RIGHT: Chains in an assortment of metals and finishes

BELOW: A variety of findings including closures, jump rings, spring rings, ear wires, head pins, and pin backs

Metal

Metal is a common material in jewelry. In fact, every jewelry project in this book includes metal. It usually comes in the form of sheet, wire, and tubing (see photo, page 12). If precious metals such as silver and gold seem too expensive and intimidating, try base metals such as brass, copper, aluminum, or salvaged "tin" from cans (made of an iron-based alloy). Coated copper wire comes in a rainbow of colors. The gauge of a metal is a value that indicates its thickness: the smaller the gauge, the thicker the metal.

Findings

The working parts that make jewelry pieces functional and wearable are called *findings.* They include closures and clasps for necklaces and bracelets, jump rings, spring rings, head pins, buckles, ear wires and posts, pin backs and stems, pendant bails, and chains. Commercially mass-produced findings are readily available in a variety of metals. You can also make your own from sheet metal or wire.

Hammers and Mallets

In jewelry making, hammers are used to shape metal, set rivets, and drive nails. You might think of a *mallet* as a softer hammer made of rubber, wood, plastic, or rawhide. Mallets shape and flatten metal without marring its surface. These tools come in many shapes and sizes intended for different purposes. Choosing the right hammer or mallet for you can largely be a matter of preference. Several of my favorites are shown on page 12, including a watchmaker's hammer with a tiny, flat head I find great for setting small rivets, and a dual-head rubber and plastic mallet.

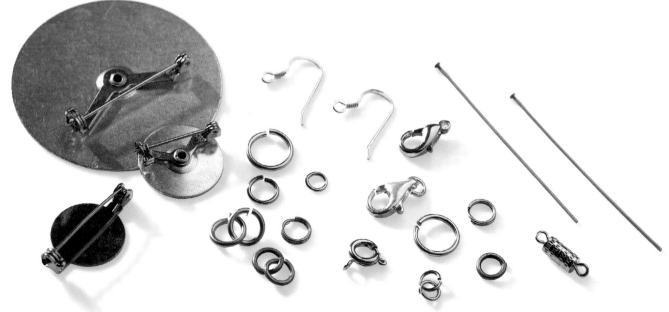

Blocks and Anvils

Most jewelry artists work at a bench or table, but they also use a variety of smaller wood and metal surfaces on which to hammer, shape, and work metal. A *bench block* is a hardened steel block that can be either sourced from steel scrap, like the one pictured at right, or purchased commercially. An *anvil* is a uniquely shaped steel block associated with blacksmithing. A *bench pin* is a piece of hardwood that gets secured to the surface of a workbench. Its notched shape provides support while sawing metal. Scrap wood blocks also come in handy while stamping or drilling metal. *Mandrels* are shaped wood and metal objects commonly used for forming rings, bracelets, and bezels.

Scissors and Shears

Metal shears are invaluable for cutting sheet metal. They come with both serrated blades, which leave behind marks on the metal, and non-serrated blades, which do not. Thin metals such as decorative "tin" from cans and aluminum flashing can be cut with scissors. Designate and label individual pairs of scissors for cutting only one specific material (paper, fabric, or metal). Keep scissors clean and sharp using a scissor sharpener.

Pliers and Cutters

Pliers are used to shape and hold wire and small pieces of metal. They are often named for the shape of their nose or their function. As the name implies, *wire cutters* are used to cut wire. *Flush cutters* make flush, or straight, cuts in wire.

Drills and Punches

Many jewelry-making tasks require that a hole be made in metal or other materials. Holes can be drilled using a hand drill (see page 18) or motor-driven electrical drill such as a rotary tool or flexible shaft machine. Holes can also be punched using a punch. *Drill bits*, which are inserted in a drill, come in a wide range of sizes for drilling holes of different sizes. A drill gauge is used to identify drill bit sizes. Special drill bits called *burs* are also used to cut and shape metal. A *pin vise* is like a small hand drill and is useful for drilling or enlarging holes in small objects, such as pearls. A *center punch* or *awl* is used to make a small depression in

metal prior to drilling. Also, when hammered, an awl or needle tool can be used to punch holes in thin gauge metal. Safety glasses should be worn during drilling or whenever flying metal or other material poses a hazard to eyes.

Saws and Blades

To cut any metal in an intricate pattern or metal that is too heavy in gauge for shears or scissors, you use a *jeweler's saw*. A jeweler's saw consists of a saw frame into which a saw blade is inserted. Blades are available in a range of qualities and sizes. A lubricant such as beeswax is used on saw blades when sawing (as well as on drill bits when drilling).

Stamping Tools

Patterns are impressed, or stamped, into metal by striking the top of a tool called a *stamp* (also referred to as a *punch* or *chasing tool*). You can adapt tools you have on hand, such as a screwdriver or nail set tool for this purpose, or you can purchase manufactured stamps. Popular stamp designs include lines, letters, and numbers, as well as figurative patterns such as flowers and leaves.

Clamps and Vises

While working metal or other materials, it is often necessary to secure one or more pieces to the work surface or to hold multiple pieces together. *Clamps* are used for this purpose, and they come in many sizes and materials. Look for those with rubber- or plastic-covered jaws that don't

damage the surfaces of objects and those with easy grip and release capabilities. Small bench vises and handheld locking pliers are also helpful for holding jewelry work.

Files and Abrasive Materials

Once cut with shears or a saw, the rough edges on metal need to be refined using *files* (see page 23). These tools come in a variety of shapes and a range of sizes, usually with separate handles. In a pinch, an emery board can sometimes fill in for a small file. To smooth or remove scratches from metal and wood, steel wool and sandpaper are used. Both are available in a range of grits or grades from super fine to extra coarse. A kitchen scouring pad can also be used.

Rivets, Eyelets, and Screws

Layers of metal are sometimes joined with *rivets,* which are small rods or tubes of metal. To hold the layers together, rivets are flared at either end. You can either make your own rivets out of wire, use nails or nail-shaped objects (such as brads and tacks) as rivets, or use commercially manufactured rivets like those pictured on page 17. *Eyelets* are a type of tube rivet, and they are set with a flaring tool called an *eyelet setter*. Other kinds of rivets include *pop rivets* and *split rivet*s. Tiny screws or bolts with nuts can also be used to join pieces of wood and metal. Rivets, eyelets, and screws are some of the many forms of jewelry attachments known as *cold connections.*

LEFT: A darkened brass finish produced by using patina solution

RIGHT (Clockwise from left): Assorted nails and brads, eyelet setter, rivets, eyelets

Soldering Supplies

During soldering, metal called *solder* is melted to join two surfaces. The heat used to melt the solder is provided by a soldering iron or torch (shown below). *Flux*, in the form of a liquid, gel, or paste, is applied to help solder flow. Other supplies needed for soldering include a striker and heat-resistant soldering surface.

Paper and Fabric Collage Supplies

There is a tremendous variety of paper and fabric available for use in collage jewelry. For cutting these materials, individual pairs of scissors should be designated and labeled. A utility knife with replacement blades can also be used. A *bone folder* is useful for burnishing, folding, and flattening paper, tape, and thin metal. Other handy supplies for collage include adhesives such as gel medium and PVA glue and brushes for applying them, as well as paints and colored pencils.

Glass and Plastic

Sheet glass and plastic can be cut and used as design elements or protective surfaces in collage. *Acrylic* is a clear or colored plastic that can be cut into shapes with a jewelry saw. *Epoxy resin* is another form of plastic. It consists of a liquid resin and a liquid hardener that, once mixed, can be poured onto a collage surface and left to harden and seal the collage.

Patina Solutions

The surface color of metal can be changed by applying a *patina solution* to the metal. Patina solutions are used to help a pattern stamped in metal to stand out or to lend shiny new metal objects a darkened, aged appearance. These solutions are made with a variety of chemicals and work on different metals, including steel, silver, copper, brass, and aluminum. Some of the many patina solutions commercially available include liver of sulfur, which makes copper and sterling silver appear brown or gray, and "gun blue," used to give steel and other metals a bluish-black appearance. Antiquing mediums and paint can also be brushed on and partially wiped off metal, wood, and other surfaces for an antiqued effect.

techniques

EVERY ARTIST NEEDS TO MASTER a set of basic skills to create their art. To that end, this chapter covers some basic techniques used in the upcoming collage jewelry projects and lists possible tools needed for those techniques. It is not intended to be an all-inclusive jewelry techniques manual, however. For additional techniques and more detailed descriptions, I refer you to some of the excellent jewelry resources available at your local library or bookstore, including *The Complete Metalsmith* and *Jewelry: Fundamentals of Metalsmithing*, both by Tim McCreight, and *The Art & Craft of Making Jewelry* by Joanna Gollberg.

Keep in mind that there simply is no substitute for hands-on experience. I highly recommend you take a jewelry-making class or workshop, particularly to learn advanced jewelry techniques such as how to solder silver (and other metals) and make bezels.

Drilling

Whatever material you use to make jewelry, whether it be metal, wood, plastic, or another material, you will very likely need to drill a hole in that material. Drilling is one of the most useful jewelry-making techniques. The instructions below describe how to drill a hole in metal.

Drilling Kit
- Drill, such as hand drill, electric drill, or drill press
- Drill bits
- Beeswax or other lubricant
- Clamps
- Center punch, awl, or needle tool
- Safety glasses
- Drilling work surface, such as bench pin or scrap wood

1. On the piece to be drilled, use a black permanent marker with an ultrafine point to mark the location of the hole to be drilled. Place the piece on a bench block, and using a center punch or awl, hammer a small depression, or dimple, into the metal at the mark.
2. Clamp the piece securely to the work surface, whether you are drilling a single layer or multiple layers, so that it will not spin while being drilled (spinning metal can cut you).
3. Insert and tightly secure a drill bit in the drill. Dip the end of the bit in beeswax or another lubricant to help prevent the bit from overheating from friction. If using a hand drill, brace your elbows on the work bench for stability, bring the drill bit to the dimple, and begin turning the drill handle. Keep turning the handle slowly and steadily, letting the spinning bit do the cutting rather than pushing the bit down into the metal. (If using an electric drill, turn on the drill to start the bit

Metal layers riveted together

Riveting Metal

Once you drill holes in two pieces of metal, you can use a rivet to attach them. A rivet can be inserted in the holes and set by spreading out the rivet on either end.

Riveting Kit
- Rivets or wire
- Bench vise
- Rivet hammer with small head, such as ball peen or watchmaker's hammer
- Flat steel surface, such as bench block
- Flush cutter (or jeweler's saw and small file)

1. Choose the rivets you will use, or make your own rivets (see step 8). You want the rivets to fit snugly in their holes, so choose a drill bit that is the same size (in diameter) or slightly smaller than your rivets. Follow the instructions on pages 18–19 to mark and drill all the holes for the rivets in the top metal piece only.

2. Position the two metal layers together and mark (with an ultrafine-point marker or awl) through one of the holes in the top layer the position of the bottom layer's matching hole. Remove the top piece and drill the marked hole in the bottom piece.

3. If you wish to create a *countersink* (or beveled hole) so that the rivet will sit flush or level within the hole, place in that hole a drill bit that is 1 or 2 sizes larger than the bit you used to drill the hole. Hand-twist the bit several times to widen the surface of the hole. (You can also use an electric drill with a ball bur to create a countersink.)

4. Position the two metal layers together again, aligning their matching holes. Insert the rivet in the hole in the top layer and through the bottom layer. Only a tiny bit of the rivet, about half its diameter, should extend beyond the bottom layer, and this end of the rivet should be flat, not angled or pointed. If too much of the rivet sticks out or it is not flat, trim it flat using flush cutters (or cut it with a jeweler's saw and file it flat).

5. Place the two metal layers with the top layer facing down on a flat steel surface, such as a bench block. Only the top or head of the rivet should be touching the block. Carefully tap the other end of the rivet with the hammer to flare it, or spread it out. Tap until the rivet end flares enough to trap the two metal layers between either end of the rivet.

6. Repeat steps 2–5 to drill another hole in the bottom layer and set a rivet in the matching set of holes in both layers. (Note that the two layers are now attached, so you

spinning at a slow speed, then bring the bit to the dimple and gently push it into the metal.) Be sure to keep the drill bit and drill perpendicular to the surface being drilled.

Be Careful: When drilling, pull back and secure long hair. Wear safety glasses to prevent injury from flying metal or broken drill bits. The drill bit may become hot, so after drilling, let the bit cool before touching it.

4. Once you have drilled through the piece, keep the bit turning in the same direction while you pull the drill up to back it out of the metal. Do not reverse the direction you turn the handle or spin the bit. Turn off the drill.

5. To remove any metal burs in or around the drilled hole, place a drill bit that is 1 or 2 sizes larger than the bit you used in the hole. Hand-twist the bit a few times on either side of the hole.

Tip: After drilling or sawing, use nail polish remover or alcohol to remove any remaining marks made with a permanent marker on metal.

will not be able to remove and reposition the top layer.) Do this one hole and rivet at a time until all the rivets are set.

Tip: When using rivets as cold connections, be sure to always set at least two rivets in the piece to hold the layers securely together. If you use only a single rivet, the two layers will pivot around the rivet.

7. To set eyelets, follow the preceding steps, but do not strike the eyelet directly with a hammer as in step 5. Instead, strike an eyelet setter with a hammer to spread out the tubular end of the eyelet.

8. To make your own rivet, cut a length of wire flush, or flat, using a flush cutter or saw. Tightly secure most of the wire in a vise perpendicular to the vise's surface so that only the tip of the flush end, equal to about the diameter of the wire, is sticking out of the vise. Flare and shape the tip of the wire to form a dome by tapping it with the hammer. Tap all around the rim of the wire tip only, avoiding the center of the wire. Once you have formed a domed rivet head, remove the wire rivet from the vise and use like any other rivet.

Sawing Metal

Some jewelry designs for metal are too intricate to be cut with metal shears or scissors. In such cases, use a jeweler's saw. Though many find it challenging, sawing is an invaluable skill well worth mastering because, once you do, just about any metal shape will be accessible to you.

Sawing Kit
- Jeweler's saw frame
- Saw blades
- Beeswax or other lubricant

1. Secure one end of a saw blade in the upper jaw of the saw frame. The teeth of the blade should point outward away from the frame and downward toward the frame's handle. Hold the top of the frame against your work surface and push on the handle with your chest to press the arms of the frame together. While pressing, secure the other end of the saw blade in the lower jaw of the frame. Release the pressure and pluck the blade. If it makes a ringing sound, it is taut and ready for use. If it makes a dull sound, secure the blade in the frame again, this time using greater pressure, until the blade is taut.

2. Lubricate the blade by running it through beeswax or a similar lubricant. (If the blade starts to catch during sawing, repeat this step as often as needed.)

3. Using an ultrafine-point black marker, draw the design or shape to be cut on the metal. With one hand, set and hold the metal flat on the edge and over the notch of the bench pin. With the other hand, hold the saw frame by the handle, keeping the frame and blade vertical. Touch the blade to the edge of the metal and make one or more upward strokes of the saw. A tiny dent in the metal will result, into which the blade's teeth can now bite and start cutting. Move the saw up and down through the metal in a steady rhythm, using the full length of the blade and vertical strokes. Cutting will occur with each downward stroke of the blade. Follow your marked line, moving the saw only in a straight path away from you and turning the metal, not the saw, to follow curves and bends in your marker line.

OPPOSITE: Stamped copper

BELOW: Sawing tools, including a saw frame, saw blades, and beeswax

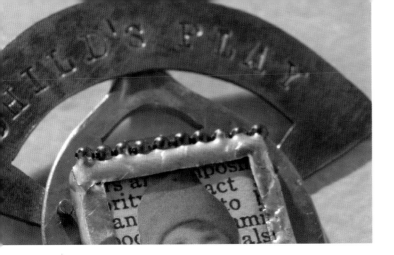

4. Saw the exterior, or perimeter shape, of the piece first, and then cut out any shapes within the piece. Sawing that is done within a piece is called *piercing* and requires that an entry hole for the saw blade be drilled first within the interior shape. Then the blade is inserted through the hole before securing the blade in the frame and sawing out the shape. After sawing, the blade is released from the frame and removed from the piece.

Tip: Don't be intimidated by the jeweler's saw, just remember that practice does make perfect. Use scrap metal to practice sawing again and again, and expect to break many blades at first. The more you practice, the easier sawing metal will become.

Stamping and Chasing Metal

The techniques of stamping and chasing can be used to add text and patterns to your collage jewelry. You might think of stamping as individual strikes and impressions, and chasing as continuous stamping that creates a series of impressions.

1. Place the metal to be stamped on a bench block. Hold the stamp in one hand, steadying the heel of your hand against the work surface. Position the patterned end of the stamp against the metal, so the tool is perpendicular to the surface of the metal.
2. Hold a hammer in your other hand, and use it to strike the top of the stamp with a single hard blow. If possible, do not strike multiple blows, which can result in multiple impressions on the metal.
3. To make additional impressions, reposition the stamp or replace it with another stamp and repeat steps 1 and 2. If necessary, use a mallet to flatten your stamped metal.

Tip: Practice on scrap metal before stamping or chasing your piece.

Experiment with how hard you strike the stamp until you are satisfied with the depth of the impression made. Experiment with the spacing and position of letters or designs. Try stamping on a different surface, such as scrap wood. You might want to use a marker to create guidelines or marks for positioning letters and words. After stamping your piece, use nail polish remover to erase the marker. Don't aim for perfection; a little variation in stamped letters and designs adds to the charm of a piece.

Wire Wrapping

The bending, wrapping, and twisting of wire for use as a cold connection is referred to as *wire wrapping*. The instructions below describe how to hang (or attach) one object with a drilled hole or gap from another object with a drilled hole or gap.

Wire Wrapping Kit
- Soft wire
- Assorted pliers, such as flat-nose, round-nose, and bent-nose
- Wire cutter
- Flush cutter

1. Use a wire cutter to cut a length of wire several inches/ 10 cm long (it is better to cut too much than too little). Straighten the wire. At about one-third of the way up the wire's length, use flat-nose pliers to bend the wire at a 90-degree angle, forming an L shape as shown on the far left in the photo on page 22.

Tip: If you don't have flat- or bent-nose pliers, try substituting whatever pliers you have on hand. If the jaws of your pliers are serrated, they may damage the surface of the wire. To prevent this, cover the serrations by wrapping the jaws with masking tape.

2. At the base of the L just below the 90-degree bend, grasp the wire with round-nose pliers. You will be using one round jaw of the pliers like a mandrel, wrapping the wire around the jaw to form a loop. Consequently, the farther back in the jaws you position the wire, the larger your loop will be. To form a loop, hold the short one-third portion of the wire, or the base of the L, and wrap it backwards tightly around one jaw of the pliers until it meets the longer two-thirds portion of wire, or the stem of the L (as shown in the photo on page 22, second from left).

*Steps in wire wrapping
a key charm*

Aging Metal

You can give metal a darkened, aged appearance by treating it with a *patina solution*. Patina solutions are mixtures of chemicals that react with metals. They vary in terms of how to use them and with what metals they react, so read and follow the manufacture's instructions. Below are general instructions that apply to several types of patina solutions.

Patina Kit
- Patina solution
- Water
- Plastic containers
- Plastic tweezers
- Paper towel
- Safety glasses
- Rubber gloves

Tip: To form multiple loops of a consistent size, use marker to mark one jaw of the round-nose pliers at the position to place the wire. Be sure to position the wire at this mark each time you wrap a loop.

3. Use your fingers to gently open the loop a bit so you can thread the object onto the wire. Seat the object in the loop, and then gently close the loop (as shown in the photo above, second from left).

4. Use bent-nose pliers with a narrow tip (or flat-nose pliers) to hold the tip of the loop closed just above the object. With your fingers, tightly wrap the short end of the wire around the longer section of the wire several times, forming tight coils (as shown on the far right in the photo above). Then use a flush cutter to trim the excess wire. Use the pliers to tuck the cut end of the wire in tightly against the coils.

Tip: If you find this step challenging, keep practicing. Try using bent-nose pliers to tighten and close up your wrapped coils and neaten up the cut wire end.

5. A short distance above the wrapped coils (about 1/8"/ 3 mm), position your flat-nose pliers and use the pliers to bend the remaining section of wire at a 90-degree angle. Repeat steps 2–4 to create a second loop and use it to attach a second object.

1. Clean the surface of the metal. If it is coated with varnish or another sealant, use steel wool to remove the coating. Once clean, avoid handling the metal.

2. If possible, immerse the metal in a patina solution. To do so, prepare a plastic container filled with just enough water to immerse one or more metal pieces. Pour a few drops of undiluted patina solution into the container.

Tip: The weaker you make the water and patina solution, the longer it will take the metal to react and change color. A slow reaction can be an advantage, allowing you time to remove the metal before it gets too dark. If the metal is not reacting in a weak solution, you can add more patina solution. For a very dark color and fast reaction, you can even use undiluted patina solution without mixing it with water. If you cannot immerse the metal, you can brush or wipe the patina solution on the metal.

ABOVE: Filed and finished silver and tin rings
OPPOSITE, BOTTOM: Beads attached by wire wrapping

Filing and Finishing Metal

Cutting and working metal leaves behind rough edges and irregular surfaces that need to be refined and finished. There is no single correct way to finish a piece of metal jewelry, though most metal work includes some filing.

Finishing Kit
- Assorted files, large and small
- Assorted grades of steel wool
- Kitchen scouring pad
- Assorted grits of sandpaper

1. Like saw blades, files are covered with tiny teeth. When pushed (not pulled) against metal, they cut and remove bits of the metal. Hold the piece against a work surface or bench pin, not up in the air. Push the file away from you and against the surface or edge of the metal using one continuous stroke. When you pull the file back toward you, lift it slightly off the metal. Continue pushing and then lifting and pulling the file as needed.

2. To refine and smooth the metal, use a range of file sizes, starting with a larger file and progressively working down to smaller files.

Tip: When smoothing the edges of very thin metal such as aluminum flashing or tin sheet, I find it easier to use a small, flexible emery board rather than a file.

3. After filing, you can also rub the surface of metal with steel wood or sand paper to further refine it. As with files, use a range of steel wool grades (or sandpaper grits),

3. Use plastic tweezers to carefully place the metal in the solution, and then watch for it to change color. Before it becomes darker than you would like, use the tweezers to remove the metal and rinse it off immediately in a water bath. If your metal is not dark enough, repeat this step until it reaches the desired color.

Be Careful: Follow the manufacturer's instructions for the safe use of a patina solution. Work in a well-ventilated area. Wear safety glasses and rubber gloves. If you pour the solution down the drain, be sure to flush your drain well by running water for several minutes (metal drainage pipes can be damaged by patina solution).

4. Place the rinsed metal on a paper towel and allow it to air dry. If the metal appears too dark, or to make letters or patterns stamped in the metal stand out, use a light hand to remove some of patina with steel wool or a kitchen scouring pad.

starting with a coarser grade (or grit) and progressively working down to a finer grade (or grit). To create a matte finish on metal, use medium grade steel wool or a kitchen scouring pad, rubbing in a circular motion.

4. There are many ways to finish metal, so let what complements your materials and piece be your guide. I often want to leave undisturbed or even preserve the original aged or patinated finish on a found object. As a preservative measure, I might apply a sealant such as wax polish, using a soft cloth to rub on a small amount, and then gently buff the surface. On the rare occasions when I want to remove tarnish and shine silver, I use a pretreated polishing cloth or soft cotton rag and metal polish. After soldering metal, Kristin Diener cleans her piece by placing it in pickle (see page 133). She polishes the metal using a buffing machine and an abrasive compound, and then goes over the piece with a soft cloth and polishing compound. Phoenix Forrester cleans and polishes her silver by tumbling it for 24 hours in a rotary tumbler along with water, dish detergent, a burnishing compound, and steel shot.

Paper Collage

Paper is a common material in collage jewelry. For the best results, take the time to learn a few simple techniques for collaging paper. Many of the techniques below can also be applied to fabric collage.

Paper Collage Kit
- Acrylic gel medium, PVA glue, or other paper adhesive
- Assorted size paintbrushes
- Container with water
- Waxed paper
- Sponge
- Small, sharp paper scissors (for detail cutting)
- Large paper scissors (or utility knife and self-healing cutting mat)

1. When designing a paper collage for jewelry, you are most likely working at a very small scale, so it is best to keep your design simple. I often choose a photo or image of a person as the focal point. I cut the image out to remove its existing background (which can distract your eye from the focal point), and then place it on a simple contrasting background paper, such as a page of small-scale text or script.

Tip: Wash your hands before handling collage paper. Then, wash them again before you begin to adhere the paper.

2. If you would prefer not to use an original paper item such as a family photo, duplicate it using either a photocopier or your computer's scanner, imaging software, and printer. Imaging software can also be used to isolate, resize, and enhance images, after which they can be printed on a variety of papers.

3. To crisply and accurately cut out detailed shapes in paper, such as the outline of a person, use small, sharp scissors. Cut with the paper deep inside the jaws of the scissors, pivoting the paper rather than the scissors as you cut curves and sharp bends.

4. Position the cutout focal image on the background paper. If the white of the cut paper visually stands out around the edges of a colored focal image when placed against the background, mask it by darkening the edges with a black or other colored pencil that matches the image or background. For example, with a sepia-toned photo, use a brown pencil; for a colored image on a black background, try using a black pencil.

Tip: For a more interesting collage composition, try offsetting rather than centering the focal image.

5. Use paper adhesive to adhere the focal image to the background paper. Some of the many kinds of paper adhesive you might find useful include acrylic gel medium (matte or gloss), heavy gel medium (matte), PVA glue (including archival glue), and glue stick. To apply the adhesive, I work on a firm surface that is dust free and covered with waxed paper. I place the focal image face down on the waxed paper, dip a damp brush in the adhesive, and lightly and quickly brush the adhesive on the paper, working from the center outward (to avoid pushing adhesive under the edge). Keep a damp sponge nearby to clean adhesive from your fingers. Then, carefully place the focal image adhesive-side down on the background paper. Cover the collage with waxed paper and carefully press the layers together with your fingers, removing any air pockets caught between the layers. Remove the waxed paper and use the sponge to gently dab up any excess adhesive on the collage before it dries.

6. Let the adhesive dry. To keep it from curling as it dries, sandwich the collage between pieces of waxed paper and weight it down under a stack of books. Once dry, use scissors to cut the collage to size. If your paper collage will not be covered by glass or plastic, seal it with a protective coating of gel medium or other sealant.

Polished silver bracelet

Using Resin

If you want to seal or embed a collage in a thick plastic coating that fills found objects and molds to any shape, epoxy resin is for you. Resin can be a bit fickle, but it can also be very fun to use.

Resin Kit
- Two-part epoxy resin
- Disposable graduated measuring cup
- Wood stirrer
- Squeeze bottle or dropper
- Safety glasses
- Rubber gloves

1. Prepare and adhere collages inside containers, such as watch cases or bezel cups, that will hold the liquid resin without leaking. Lay the containers on a flat, level surface in a location that is dust free and where the containers will not be disturbed. (Irregularly shaped containers, such as shells, can be leveled by placing them on the surface of a bowl filled with rice or coarse sand.)
2. Mix the resin according to the manufacturer's instructions. Using a disposable graduated measuring cup, pour the required amount of liquid resin in the cup, and on top of that add the required amount of liquid hardener. It is essential that your measurements be precise or the resin will not harden. Only pour out as much resin and hardener as you are likely to use, so none of it goes to waste. Use a clean wood stirrer to gently but thoroughly mix the liquids, minimizing the amount of air you mix in. Once mixed, pour the resin into a squeeze bottle with a small opening.

Be Careful: Follow the manufacturer's instructions for the safe use of epoxy resin. Work in a well-ventilated area. Wear safety glasses and rubber gloves.

3. Fill the container with resin a few drops at a time, letting the resin spread and settle before adding more drops. If bubbles form in the resin, disperse them by opening your mouth and gently exhaling on them. Alternatively, try directing air from a craft heat gun onto the surface of the resin.
4. Allow the resin to set overnight or until solid.

Tip: Learn to live with a few bubbles in your resin, because some are inevitable. You can mask bubbles by adding micro glitter to the resin while wet, as Phoenix Forrester does (see page 112). Or, think of the bubbles as "happy accidents" that can lead to a more interesting design. Stephanie Rubiano likes to cover bubbles by gluing crystals and other embellishment to the resin surface (see page 94).

Cutting Glass

Collages made of fragile materials like paper and fabric last longer when encased beneath glass. Once you learn to cut glass yourself, you'll have ready access to pieces custom-sized to match the dimensions of your collage jewelry.

Glass Cutting Kit
- Safety glasses
- Glass
- Glass cutter
- Running pliers
- Glass cutter oil or other lubricant
- Small cork-backed metal ruler
- Permanent marker
- Thin double-sided tape (such as poster tape)
- Glass cleaner
- Paper towels

1. Use glass cleaner to clean the glass. Measure and mark a cutting line using a ruler and marker.

Be Careful: Use caution when cutting and handling glass. Wear eye protection. Avoid touching the sharp edges. Work on newspaper to catch glass chips, and immediately dispose of the paper and any broken glass safely.

2. Place the glass on a flat, hard, work surface covered with newspaper. Use glass cutter oil to lubricate the cutting wheel of the glass cutter. (I use an ordinary hardware store glass cutter. I lightly soak a cotton ball in oil and run the wheel through the ball before each cut.)

3. Place the ruler cork-side down on the glass parallel to the marked line. Holding the glass cutter upright against the ruler edge with the wheel at one end of the cutting line, score the glass by applying even pressure and drawing the cutter toward you or away from you (the latter works best for me). Score along the entire length of the cutting line in one continuous motion. Press firmly with the cutter so you hear a scratching sound, but not so hard that you break the glass. Score the glass only once.

Tip: Before making each cut, use a fresh piece of thin double-sided tape to adhere the cork back of the ruler to the glass and keep the ruler from slipping as you score.

4. With the ball end of the cutter, gently tap the underside of the score. This perpetuates the score throughout the glass's thickness. The glass may just break in two. If not, position the tip of running pliers at one end of the score, lining up the center of the pliers with the score line. Gently squeeze the pliers closed until the glass breaks along the length of the score. Carefully clean the cut glass.

Tip: If you prefer not to attempt cutting glass, you can have a local glazier cut glass for you.

Soldering Glass

Although two pieces of glass can't be soldered together, two thin pieces of copper can be. By adhering copper foil tape to the glass, soldering can be used to join two pieces of stacked glass to make a charm.

Soldering Kit
- Flux
- Flux brush
- Wire solder
- Soldering iron
- Copper foil tape
- Small spring clamps
- Scissors
- Flux remover

1. Cut and clean two matching pieces of glass (as described on page 27). Place two images (cut to size and back-to-back) between the pieces of glass. Use a small spring clamp (shown at right) to hold all the layers together. Remember to be careful when handing cut glass.
2. Cut a piece of copper foil tape long enough to go around the perimeter of the glass charm and overlap itself a little.

Tip: Since I use very thin glass that is only about $1/32$"/1.8 mm thick, I prefer to use $3/16$"/5 mm, or even $1/4$"/6 mm, width copper foil tape (black backed). If you are in doubt about the width of the tape to buy, I suggest getting $1/4$"/6 mm or wider tape, which you can always trim down with a utility knife. If possible, use foil tape that is black on the sticky back side; black will be less distracting if visible than another color.

3. Wrap the foil around the edges of the charm, centering the edge within the strip of foil tape. To do so, remove just enough of the tape backing to cover one edge at a time, center the edge within the strip of foil tape, and then press on the tape. Continue in this manner until you have wrapped the foil around all four edges of the charm, repositioning the clamp as needed. Be sure to overlap the two ends of the tape away from the corners of the charm. Snip the tape at the corners and miter the tape corners. Use a bone folder to press down, or burnish, and securely adhere the tape along the edges and over onto the face of the glass, on the front and back. Take your time on this step, because good adhesion is essential.

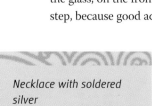

Necklace with soldered silver

Tip: My favorite pressing tool is my thumbnail. To ensure good adhesion, I press all over the copper foil tape with my thumbnail.

4. Work on a heat-resistant surface, such as an old ceramic tile. Heat the soldering iron according to the manufacturer's instructions. Brush flux on the copper foil only, using the flux sparingly. When heated, touch the tip of the soldering iron to the solder and use the tip to spread the melted solder over the copper foil. Do not touch the charm, which will be hot, but lay it flat on the tile or use one or two small spring clamps with the rubber tips removed to help you hold and maneuver the charm as you solder it. While soldering, remove solder buildup on the tip of the iron by periodically wiping the tip on a damp sponge. Continue spreading solder one edge at a time until all the copper tape is covered with solder.
5. Shut off the soldering iron and let it cool. Let the charm cool completely before handling it. Carefully wipe down the soldered area with flux remover applied to a soft cloth to remove any flux remaining on the piece.

Soldering Silver

This advanced technique is best learned from an expert in a classroom setting. Once you master it, you might want to gather the tools listed next.

Advanced Soldering Kit
- Torch (such as acetylene)
- Hard, medium, and easy wire silver solder
- Striker
- Soldering surface, such as heat-resistant ceramic or charcoal block
- Wire cutter
- Flux
- Brush
- Stainless steel tweezers

YOU DON'T HAVE TO BE a mathematician or code breaker to relate to numbers. The time of day your child was born, the street number of the house where you grew up, your lucky number or birth date—numbers have a certain sentimental power for us all.

So do letters or words, such as a loved one's name, your spouse's initials, or perhaps your apartment address. If you grew up reading detective stories, the name Sherlock or the address 221B will likely bring back memories.

The projects in this chapter explore ways of using numbers and letters in collage jewelry to symbolize events, times, and places in your life. Think of an individual number or a combination of numbers and letters with personal meaning. You might recall an important date, your age when a milestone was reached, a child or parent's birth year, a friend's initials, or a street address. That number can be collaged with other materials, such as family photos, to create a very personal keepsake.

House, room, and sign numbers like those pictured on page 30 have great potential as raw materials for collage. They come in a vast array of sizes and materials, including brass, aluminum, plastic, and wood. Hardware stores and home-improvement centers generally have a selection of new numbers in stock. I keep an eye open for vintage numbers at antique stores and flea markets.

And what would games be without numbers? Game pieces such as dice, dominoes, bingo and lotto pieces, and Scrabble and Anagrams tiles display numbers, letters, and symbols (dots) galore. Numbers are also found on the paper components of games, including game boards, money, spinners, and cards. Also, you can search out old license plates, vintage locker tags, new brass number charms, and rulers to use in your own one-of-a-kind numerical collage jewelry.

Do you remember when arcades and tourist destinations had machines like photo booths and key chain laminators for transforming travel memories into kitschy souvenirs? One such machine provided round aluminum disks, or good luck "coins," into which you stamped any combination of numbers and letters you wished. The stamped message might be an easily recognized name or date or even a secret combination of numbers and letters decipherable only by its tourist creator. The one I made as a child is stamped with a jumble of numbers and letters, the meaning of which only my younger self knows for sure, but it still conjures up a few fond memories.

Like kitschy arcade souvenirs, your collage jewelry can count out or spell out memories with numbers and letters. Whether your numerical message is easily understood or as cryptic as the secret code on my childhood souvenir, why not give one of these jewelry projects a try?

"I keep an eye open for vintage numbers at antique stores and flea markets."

domino necklace

Artist: **Janette Schuster**

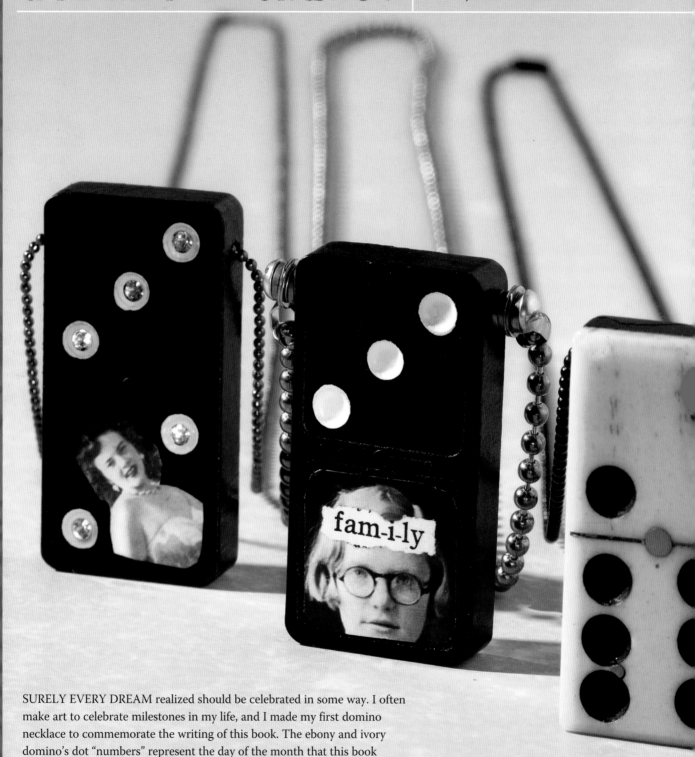

SURELY EVERY DREAM realized should be celebrated in some way. I often make art to celebrate milestones in my life, and I made my first domino necklace to commemorate the writing of this book. The ebony and ivory domino's dot "numbers" represent the day of the month that this book became a part of my life. On the back, I included my own secret message, the word for "book" in a language my grandfather spoke but I have yet to master.

Materials

- Domino, antique ebony and ivory (approximately 2 x 1 x ⅜"/5 x 2.5 x 1 cm)
- Tintype
- Text from book
- ¼"/6 mm x #20 brass escutcheon pins or nails
- Acrylic gloss medium
- #1, #2, or #3 ball (or bead) chain, 36"/91 cm in black or color of your choice
- Matching ball chain connector

Tools and Supplies

- Pencil or marker
- Drilling kit (drill press or hand drill) with ⁵/₆₄"/2 mm, #59, and #71 drill bits
- Small file
- Steel wool
- Mallet
- Thin double-sided tape (such as poster tape)
- Paper collage kit
- Small paintbrush

Optional

- Wire cutters
- Opaque fine-point marker in white or light color

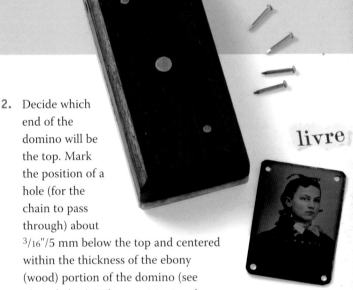

MAKE IT YOUR OWN

To make your own version, you can use several kinds of game pieces that might already be in your family treasure trove, including vintage or modern dominoes, dice, and mahjong tiles made of plastic or wood. Choose numbers, photos, and words to use that have personal significance to you. If using plastic game pieces, you'll need to glue on rather than nail in the tintype.

Ebony and Ivory Domino

1. Choose a domino. I look for vintage ones with a timeworn appearance. Keep an eye out for vintage game pieces at yard sales, flea markets, online auctions, and antique stores. Individual pieces or incomplete sets can sometimes be had for a song. New dominoes can also be used.

2. Decide which end of the domino will be the top. Mark the position of a hole (for the chain to pass through) about ³/₁₆"/5 mm below the top and centered within the thickness of the ebony (wood) portion of the domino (see photo below). When positioning the hole for drilling (and the tintype in step 5), take note of the location of any rivets holding the domino together and adjust the position to avoid hitting the rivets. Use an awl to make a dimple at the mark before drilling. Use the smallest drill bit possible to drill a hole large enough for the chain to pass through and move freely. I used a ⁵/₆₄"/2 mm drill bit in a drill press. A hand drill can also be used, but a drill press makes it easier to drill a hole parallel to the top edge of the domino. If you are using a plastic domino, such as a vintage Bakelite domino, drill slowly to avoid overheating and melting the plastic around your drill bit.

3. Select a tintype (a photograph printed on sheet metal) and trim it, if necessary, to fit part of the back of the domino. Use a small file and steel wool to gently blunt and round any sharp metal edges that might snag on clothing.

4. At the four corners of the tintype, gently dimple and drill holes using a #59 drill bit (see photo above). Be sure to clamp near the dimple location, because the thin metal deforms easily during drilling. If it does become

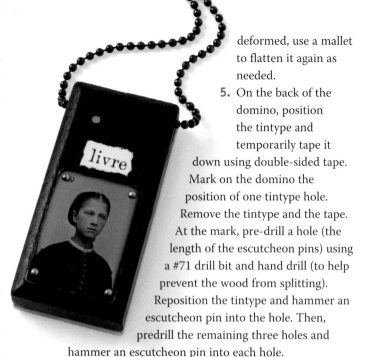

deformed, use a mallet to flatten it again as needed.

5. On the back of the domino, position the tintype and temporarily tape it down using double-sided tape. Mark on the domino the position of one tintype hole. Remove the tintype and the tape. At the mark, pre-drill a hole (the length of the escutcheon pins) using a #71 drill bit and hand drill (to help prevent the wood from splitting). Reposition the tintype and hammer an escutcheon pin into the hole. Then, predrill the remaining three holes and hammer an escutcheon pin into each hole.

6. Find a word or phrase with meaning to you in a damaged antique book and gently tear it out. I chose a word from a late Victorian children's book of perhaps the same age as the domino. Placing the word on the back gives it the subtlety of a secret message for the wearer, one usually hidden from view. Glue the paper to the domino (see photo above) and let the adhesive dry. For durability, seal the paper with several coats of gloss medium.

Tip: Using materials of a similar antiquity—like the ivory domino, tintype, and text—can lend authenticity to a new collage piece. Alternatively, juxtaposing items of different vintages, like modern rhinestones and an old photo, can add some quirky flavor.

7. The timeworn beauty and graphic punch of the ivory front of this domino require no more adornment than a simple black ball chain. Ball chain, also know as bead chain, comes in a rainbow of colors and a range of ball sizes. (I particularly like the smaller and harder-to-find sizes #1 and #2 in metallic and black finishes; ball chain in sizes #3 and larger are commonly found in hardware stores.) I made this necklace very long, about "flapper" length, so that it swings freely when worn. However, you can use wire cutters to cut the chain to any desired length. Thread the ball chain through the hole and attach the ends of the chain with a matching connector. If you wish, sign your piece with an opaque marker in white or another light color.

Family Domino Variation

The foundation of the domino necklace offers the possibility for many personalized variations. Here is a different version that might help jumpstart your own creativity.

Additional Materials

- Domino, vintage hardwood (approximately 2 x 1 x $\frac{5}{16}$"/ 5 x 2.5 x .8 cm)
- Photo
- Text from dictionary
- Two $\frac{1}{8}$"/3 mm brass eye connectors
- #6 ball (or bead) chain, 36"/91 cm in brass or color of your choice
- Two #4 x $\frac{1}{2}$"/13 mm round-head brass wood screws
- Screwdriver
- Heishi beads or small washers (optional)

1. Choose a domino without any dots on one half (see page 34, bottom). Plan a collage to fit within the area without dots. Cut out a photo to fit, and tear out a word with personal meaning from a vintage dictionary. Do not adhere the collage until after steps 2 and 3 (to minimize damage to the collage).
2. Decide which end of the domino will be the top. On either side, mark the position of each screw about $3/16$"/5 mm below the top and centered within the thickness of the domino. Use an awl to make a dimple at each mark before drilling. At each dimple, drill a short hole using a $5/64$"/2 mm drill bit and a hand drill. Don't drill all the way through the domino; just drill about $1/4$"/6 mm deep.
3. Onto the first screw thread one heishi bead, an eye connector, and then two more heishi beads (or if you prefer, just use the eye connector). Use a screwdriver to attach the screw in the drill hole. Don't overtighten the screw, since you want the connector and chain to move freely. Repeat this step for the second screw (see photo below).

Tip: Clamp the domino down while attaching each screw.

4. Glue the collage to the domino and let the adhesive dry. For durability, seal the paper with several coats of gloss medium.
5. Snap each end of the ball chain into a connector. If you wish, sign your piece with an opaque maker in white or another light color.

Resin and Rhinestone Domino Variation

Here's another variation on the domino theme, using resin and rhinestones.

Additional Materials

- Domino, vintage hardwood (approximately 2 x 1 x $5/16$"/ 5 x 2.5 x .8 cm)
- #1, #2, or #3 ball (or bead) chain, 36"/91 cm in aged copper or color of your choice
- Matching ball chain connector
- Rhinestones
- Photo
- Resin kit
- Straight pin

1. Choose a domino with some open space on one half. Cut out a photo to fit within the open space. Do not adhere the photo until after step 2 (to minimize damage to the collage). Use an awl to create deeper indentations in the dots, in which rhinestone points will sit.
2. Repeat step 2 of the Ebony and Ivory Domino instructions (on page 33) to drill the domino all the way through.
3. Glue the photo to the domino within the open space, and glue the rhinestones within the dots (see photo below). Let the adhesive dry.
4. Follow the instructions for using resin on page 26. Pour a minimal amount of resin, perhaps a drop or two, into each domino recess. If you add too much resin, it will overflow the recess. Use a straight pin to help spread the resin. Wait a few minutes, and then add more resin if needed. Let the resin dry until hard.
5. Thread the ball chain through the hole and attach the ends of the chain with a matching connector. If you wish, sign your piece with an opaque maker in white or another light color.

stencil bangle

Artist: **Janette Schuster**

MY FIRST EXPEDITION to the famed Brimfield antique flea market netted me some amazing finds, including a box of vintage brass stencils. While poring over these graphic treasures, it occurred to me that their flexibility and ability to interconnect makes them ideal ingredients for a bangle-style bracelet. I chose an assortment of letters and numbers with meaning to me and created a wearable souvenir of a successful day of treasure hunting.

Materials

- Interlocking brass stencils, vintage or new
- Photos
- Two sheets thin transparency plastic
- Black acrylic paint, or color of your choice
- Glue stick
- 1/16"/1.5 mm brass (or gold colored) eyelets

Tools and Supplies

- Cloth or paper towel
- Small-nose pliers
- Small file
- Steel wool or scouring pad
- Mallet
- Sharp paper scissors
- Masking tape
- Paintbrush
- Ultrafine-point permanent black marker
- 1/16"/1.5 mm metal punch
- Eyelet setter
- Hammer
- Bench block

Optional

- Patina kit
- Clear nail polish, wax, or spray-on sealant
- Old credit card or scrap plastic
- Awl
- Pen or marker
- Scrap of paper
- Photocopier or computer with imaging software, scanner, and printer

MAKE IT YOUR OWN

To make your own version, use a combination of stencil numbers and letters with personal significance. If you wish, spell out words or a phrase with the stencils. Collage them with photos of family or friends. Instead of black, use your favorite color to paint the background. I like the contrast of shiny new eyelets and aged brass stencils, but you can use a patina solution on the eyelets to darken their appearance before setting them.

1. Choose an assortment of stencil numbers and letters. Interlock the stencils to form a bangle and try it on for size. You should be able to easily slide your hand in and out of the bangle, but the fit should be tight enough that the bangle does not slip off while wearing it. If the fit isn't right, try adding or removing one stencil at a time, or substituting stencils of different widths.

Tip: Stencils vary. Some seem to form a more circular bangle if you connect them wrong side up (letters backward).

2. Use a damp cloth to clean the stencils. Resist the temptation to chip off the existing paint.

Be Careful: Leave old paint intact. Old paint may contain lead, which can have adverse health effects if inhaled or ingested.

3. Make sure the interlocking tracks slide freely. If necessary, use pliers to bend back any misaligned tracks. Then, use a small file and steel wool to smooth any sharp edges on the stencils. Use a mallet to flatten any misshapen stencils.

4. If you are using new stencils, you might want to age the shiny brass with a patina solution (see the instructions on page 22).

5. Choose an assortment of photos of people to collage behind the stencils. To help make the composition of the bangle a bit more interesting, vary the size and position of the photos as well as their orientation (i.e., the direction in which the people pictured are facing).

Consider leaving plenty of blank space around the photos to help the outlines of the numbers and letters stand out. Use your computer's imaging software or a photocopier to adjust the size and color of the photos as desired. (For example, you may wish to make black-and-white photos sepia toned.)

6. Cut out the outline of the people in the photos. Temporarily tape them into position behind the stencils to test the composition, and then remove the tape.

7. Use steel wool or a scouring pad to scuff up a sheet of transparency plastic to give it tooth. Paint the transparency with two or more coats of acrylic paint in a contrasting color of your choice, letting the paint dry between coats. I used black paint to help the numbers, letters, and photos pop.

8. Cut a rectangle of painted transparency to fit behind each stencil. Use a dab of glue stick to adhere each photo in position on top of the painted surface. Cut matching rectangles from a sheet of unpainted transparency to place on top, in order to sandwich each photo between two transparency layers. Tack each unpainted layer onto each painted layer with a few dabs of glue stick. Tape the layers into position behind the stencils. Interlock the stencils to make sure the transparency layers don't interfere with the interlocking tracks. Trim the transparencies as needed so each track slides freely. Take the stencils apart again.

Tip: When base metals such as brass come in contact with your skin, they can react with and irritate your skin. To prevent this, consider coating any metal surface that will be touching your skin (such as the underside of the stencils) with clear nail polish, wax, or a spray-on sealant before assembling the bangle.

9. On the top of each stencil, mark the position of four holes in which eyelets will be set. You can simply eyeball their position or, for greater consistency of spacing, create a template from thin plastic (I used an old credit card) punched with an awl (see photo, page 38). Since the stencils vary in width, I marked holes a consistent distance apart and a consistent distance from the top and bottom stencil edges. For unusually narrow stencils, such as the small "c" or cents symbol, you might need to modify the template to fit. (Be sure you position your holes close enough to the edge of the stencils to use a metal punch tool, as in step 10.)

10. At one mark, use a metal punch tool to punch a $^1/_{16}$"/ 1.5 mm hole in the stencil and its transparency layers. Insert an eyelet in the hole and set it, and then punch and set the remaining three holes and eyelets. Remove the tape. Repeat this step for the remaining stencils (see photo above, top).

11. To add your signature to the bangle, sign a small scrap of paper. Use an awl to scratch out a small window from one black painted transparency. Glue the signed paper in the window (see photo above, bottom) before setting the eyelets in step 10.

our house pendant

Artist: **Janette Schuster**

GROWING UP, I LIVED AND DREAMED in a simple ranch house on a quiet dead-end street. To celebrate sharing that childhood home with the little sister who came to be my best friend, I made this pendant using a metal house number and an image of two dark-haired siblings.

Materials

- Brass house number, new
- Tintype
- Acrylic gloss medium
- One pair of brass wing stampings or charms
- 20-gauge aluminum sheet, approximately 3¼ x 2½"/8.3 x 6.4 cm
- Fine steel wool (#0000)
- Two #4-40 x ⅜"/1 cm brass round-head machine screws
- Two #4-40 x ⅜"/1 cm steel hex nuts
- 22-gauge brass sheet, approximately 1 x ¾"/2.5 x 1.9 cm
- ¼ to ½"/6 to 13 mm x #20 brass escutcheon pins
- 18-gauge brass wire
- Brass picture hanger
- Brass chain, approximately 25"/64 cm
- Two brass jump rings
- Brass watch swivel

Tools and Supplies

- Paintbrush
- Tracing or other paper
- Pencil
- Scissors
- Rubber cement
- Small clamp
- Drilling kit (drill press, electric drill, or hand drill) with ⁵⁄₆₄"/2 mm, ⁷⁄₆₄"/3 mm, and #61 drill bits
- Finishing kit
- Sawing kit
- Small file
- Ultrafine-point permanent marker
- Metal shears
- Masking or packaging tape
- Bone folder
- ³⁄₁₆"/5 mm rub-on letters, 18 pt. Helvetica or smaller type
- Moist fine- or chisel-point permanent marker
- Needle tool or book awl
- Facial tissue
- PCB etchant solution
- Two small plastic containers (for etchant and water bath)
- Water
- Paper towel
- Ammonia or baking soda
- Nail polish remover
- Respirator
- Safety glasses
- Rubber gloves
- Apron
- Patina kit
- Industrial-strength glue
- Pliers
- Screwdriver
- Wire wrapping kit
- Round-nose pliers
- Red marker or pencil
- Magnifying glass

MAKE IT YOUR OWN

To make your own version, choose a metal house, apartment, or hotel-room number based on one of the numbers in your current home or previous childhood street address. Then, look for a tintype photo to represent family members who still live or once lived there. Or, use an image of a young couple to symbolize your first home as newlyweds. Remember that you can use a new or vintage metal number; new brass numbers are readily available and can be aged to look vintage. You can also look for numbers made of aluminum, which are lighter in weight.

1. Choose a metal number. Keep in mind that numbers like 0, 4, 6, 8, and 9 are easier to use because they have an enclosed "frame" within which to place a photo. (You can still use other open numbers, such as 2 or 5, by leaving one edge of the tintype uncovered where there is no metal "frame" enclosing it.)
2. Choose a tintype and seal the surface with several coats of gloss medium. Let the medium dry between coats.
3. Lay the number faceup on tracing paper and trace around it. Decide on the position of wings or other decorative elements and trace them in position. The wings will need to be supported from behind. Inside the wing tracings, sketch wing supports that won't be visible when viewed from the front of the piece (see photo below).

Tip: Color the wing supports a bright red to help prevent you from sawing them off in step 7.

far enough from the existing hole so they (and any wire passed through them later) won't interfere with the screw head (see photo, left). Using a $5/64"$/2 mm bit and a drill press or electric drill, drill the holes. Temporarily reattach the number and aluminum backing and, drilling through the two holes in the number, drill coordinating holes in the aluminum. Unscrew the nuts and take the layers apart again.

If you wish, sign the aluminum backing at this time by stamping your name or initials in the metal.

9. Use fine steel wool to remove any varnish coating the top and sides of the number. A cloudy surface appearance indicates the varnish has been scratched but not completely removed. Be thorough, because any varnish remaining will prevent the patina solution applied in step 14 from working.

10. To make the "home" charm, use metal shears to cut a rectangle out of your brass sheet. File and finish the charm with steel wool. Place the charm just below the base of the number and on it mark the position of two holes to match the holes in the number. Drill the holes using a $5/64"$/2 mm bit.

11. Cover the back of the charm with masking or packaging tape, overlapping the pieces and burnishing them down well for good coverage. Attach extra tape on the back at either end to form long "handles" for lowering and raising the brass into and out of the etchant later on. Clean the front surface of the charm with fine steel wool and avoid touching it again.

12. Use rub-on letters to spell out "home" or another word on the surface of the charm. Follow the manufacturer's directions on the package to help you position and rub the letters securely onto the brass charm. Use a juicy new fine-point marker to cover the surface completely (including the letters) with ink. Draw the marker slowly over the surface in one direction, and avoid pulling up the marker ink by not going back over already covered areas. Let the ink dry. Twist a small piece of facial tissue between your fingers to form a soft pointed tool. Using the fine point of a needle tool (and a magnifying glass, if necessary), carefully scratch off the rub-on letters and dust off any remaining specs of letter with the tissue. Keep cleaning the tip of the needle tool. Don't aim for perfection; a little variation in the letters adds character. In step 13, the exposed brass letters will become etched by the solution and the areas covered with marker ink will remain raised.

4. Roughly cut out the tracing and use rubber cement to adhere it to the aluminum sheet. (Aluminum is the best backing metal to use because it won't add much weight to the already heavy brass number.) Let the rubber cement dry.

5. Bring your number to a hardware store, and ask for brass round-head machine screws (and matching nuts) that will fit through the existing holes in the number and are a bit longer than the combined thickness of the number and aluminum sheet. I used #4-40 × $3/8"$/1 cm brass round-head machine screws. You will need one screw and nut for each existing hole.

6. Align the number over the tracing on the aluminum and clamp together the number and aluminum. Using a $7/64"$/3 mm bit, drill into one of the existing holes in the number through the tracing and aluminum. Insert a screw in the hole, attach a nut, and tighten the nut just enough to hold the layers together. Repeat this step for all existing holes in the number.

7. Using the number and wing support tracings as a template, saw out the aluminum backing layer. File the backing layer so it will not be visible behind the number or wings when viewed from the front of the piece. Then, use steel wool to give the backing a smooth finish.

8. Unscrew the nuts, take the layers apart, and remove the tracing paper. Turn the number to the back side. At the base of the number, mark the position of two holes (from which the "home" charm will hang), preferably in a flat area well inside the thick walls of the number but

13. Pour enough etchant solution into a plastic container to just submerge the charm, and then use the tape handles to lower the charm just below the surface of the etchant and keep it level. Let the charm etch for about 1 hour, raising it every 15 minutes to check and agitate it. When it is etched to the depth desired, remove it from the etchant. Rinse the charm in a water bath, and then scrub it with ammonia or baking soda. Let it dry. Clean the marker ink off the charm with nail polish remover, and then clean the entire charm with steel wool.

Be Careful: Follow the manufacturer's instructions for safe use and disposal of etchant. Work in a well-ventilated area and avoid breathing the fumes. Avoid contact with the etchant, and wear a respirator, safety glasses, rubber gloves, and an apron. To neutralize the etchant, work outdoors and use ammonia or baking soda. Do not pour the etchant down the drain.

14. Use a patina solution (following the instructions on page 22) to give the charm, the number, and any other metals parts you desire (wings, screws, escutcheon pins, wire, and findings) an aged appearance. To make the letters on the charm stand out, gingerly clean the surface around the letters with steel wool or a kitchen scouring pad.

15. Position the tintype between the number and aluminum backing, and trim the tintype to fit if necessary. Spread a small amount of industrial strength glue on the back of the tintype and front of the aluminum backing, and press the two together. Assemble the number, tintype, and backing, and reattach them with the screws and nuts. Use pliers and a screwdriver to tighten only the bottom screw and nut.

16. Drill two holes in each of the wings using a #61 drill bit. Place one wing in position on the aluminum backing, and mark the wing's first drill hole on the aluminum. Remove the wing, drill the hole in the aluminum, and use a brass escutcheon pin to rivet the wing to the aluminum. Drill through the wing's second drill hole and through the aluminum, and rivet again. Repeat this step for the second wing.

17. Use brass wire and wire wrapping (following the instructions on page 21) to suspend the "home" charm from the base of the number.

18. To form a bale for the pendant, use round-nose pliers to bend the hooked end of a brass picture hanger to form a closed loop (as shown above). Remove the nut at the top of the pendant and thread the other end of the picture hanger on the screw so that it lies flat against the aluminum backing. Reattach the nut, but don't tighten it completely.

19. Cut the chain to the desired length. Attach a jump ring to each end of the chain, and with one jump ring attach a watch swivel to the chain. Clip the swivel to the bale and the free end of the chain to the swivel. Try on the necklace and, if necessary, rotate the bale slightly until the pendant hangs correctly (as shown below). Then, use pliers and a screwdriver to tighten the top screw and nut.

soldered charm earrings

Artist: **Janette Schuster**

MY PARENTS WOULD HAVE BEEN THRILLED to learn of my writing this book and would have bragged to everyone within earshot. I miss them, so on their wedding anniversary each year I do something to mark the day in 1953 that they began their journey through life together. This year I combined images of Mom and Dad with materials mostly from my local hardware store to create these two-sided anniversary earrings.

Materials

- Thin glass (such as slide binder glass or microscope slides), approximately 4"/10.2 cm square
- Collage papers such as photographs, letters, ephemera, etc.
- Brass nails with embossed numbered heads
- 20-gauge silver-colored wire, approximately 6"/15.2 cm
- Two sterling silver French ear wires

Tools and Supplies

- Glass cutting kit
- Glass cleaner
- Photocopier or computer with imaging software, scanner, and printer
- Paper collage kit
- Pencil
- Soldering kit
- Sawing kit
- Fine steel wool (#0000)
- Ceramic tile, recycled or new
- Double-sided foam tape
- Wire cutter
- Round-nose pliers or small mandrel
- Ultrafine-point permanent marker
- Flat-nose pliers
- Anvil or bench block
- Hammer

Optional

- Sanding block
- Utility knife

MAKE IT YOUR OWN

To make your own version, choose a four-digit number to commemorate a year important to you—that of an engagement, wedding, anniversary, or personal achievement. Or, you might celebrate the birth years of you and your spouse or of your children, parents, or grandparents. You can also use these soldered charms individually as pendants or in multiples in a charm bracelet or necklace.

1. Cut four pieces of glass (see page 27 for instructions) to the same size, about 1 × 3/4"/2.5 × 1.9 cm or any desired size suitable for earrings.
2. You might want to use a sanding block to sand the sharp edges of the glass, to prevent cuts during handling. Then, clean the cut glass with glass cleaner.
3. Choose an image for the main focus of the collage that will be on the front side of each earring. You might use one photograph for both earrings or, as I have done, use a different photograph for each earring. Use your computer's imaging software or a photocopier to adjust the color as desired and reduce the photo so that it fits within the dimensions of the cut glass. Print out each image and, using small, sharp scissors, cut them out.

Tip: When using a photocopier, how do you know how much to reduce or enlarge an image? Measure the height of the part of the image you want to include. Measure the height to which you want to reduce or enlarge the image. Then use this formula: (size of existing image/size you want image to be) x 100 = percentage to which you must enlarge or reduce image.

10. Choose four brass nails with numbers of your choice embossed on the heads. Use a jeweler's saw to cut the heads off the nails, leaving a length of nail shank equal to or a bit less than the thickness of a charm. Clean the back of each nail with steel wool.

11. To a ceramic tile, adhere pieces of double-sided foam tape in an inverted "T" pattern, similar to that shown in the bottom photo below. At the base of the inverted T, press the cut nail heads, numbered-side down, into the tape. Arrange the nail heads in a tight line so their edges are touching and, when flipped over, their embossing will read as your chosen four-digit number. Brush a small amount of flux on the backs of the nail heads and remaining shafts.

12. Brush flux on the soldered bottom and bottom front edges of one charm. Place the charm front-side down into the tape so that the bottom edge of the charm sits

4. Choose a background paper—such as a handwritten love letter or marriage certificate—that contrasts with your focal image. Use imaging software or a photocopier to reduce the background paper so that individual words or phrases fit within the dimensions of the cut glass (I reduced mine by 50 percent, as shown above). Print out the background.

5. To create two collages, use paper adhesive to adhere the images to the background paper. Let the adhesive dry.

6. Position one piece of cut glass as desired over a collage, and trace around the outside of the glass. Remove the glass and use scissors to cut out the collage just inside of the traced line. (Alternatively, as you hold the glass over the collage, cut around the edges of the glass with a utility knife.) Repeat this step for the second collage.

7. To create and cut out a new collage for the back side of each earring, repeat steps 3–6 using new photos (I used photos of my parents as children). You can also use just the background paper as the collage for the back side of each earring.

8. You should have four small collages, or two "sets" of front and back collages (see photo at right, top). Use a dab of adhesive to adhere each front collage to a back collages, back-to-back. Let the adhesive dry. Now you have a two-sided collage for each earring.

9. Clean each piece of glass again. Sandwich each two-sided collage between two pieces of glass. To form charms, tape and solder each glass "sandwich" following the instructions on page 29.

flush against the nail heads and remaining shafts. Use a piece of tape along the top edge of the charm to help anchor it snugly against the nail heads.

13. Use the soldering iron to solder the nail heads to the charm as shown in the photo at right.

14. Cut 2–3"/5–7.6 cm of silver wire from which to make an inverted "U"-shaped attachment for hanging the charm. Create a loop in the center of the length of wire by bending the wire around round-nose pliers or a small mandrel. On either side of the loop, mark a point about 3/16"/5 mm from the crest of the loop. At each mark, use flat-nose pliers to bend the wire out at a 90-degree angle. Hold one of the wire's 90-degree angles flush against the perpendicular edge of an anvil or bench block, and hammer the wire flat. Repeat this process for the wire's other 90-degree angle. Place the attachment against the top edge of the charm with the loop centered on the edge. Trim each end of the wire so the attachment is a little shorter than the top edge of the charm.

15. Brush flux on the top edge of the charm and flattened part of the attachment. Using tape and pliers to hold the attachment flush against the top edge of the charm, solder the attachment to the charm. You might need to flip the charm over and add solder to the other side. Let the charm cool, and then remove any tape clinging to it, the attachment, or the numbered nail heads. Remember to remove any remaining flux and marker.

16. Repeat steps 10–15 for the second charm. Use pliers to attach the charms to ear wires.

Double Date Earrings

The earrings (below, right) were inspired by a friend's grandparents and the years they met (1927) and married (1928). To make a similar pair, follow the steps in the previous section, but in step 10, choose a different set of numbered brass nails for each earring to represent different four-digit years.

gallery

Thomas Mann
(above)

License Plate Pin, 1990,
3¼ x 2"/ 8.2 x 5 cm.
License plate, acrylic,
brass, antique photo.

"I was intrigued with
the embossed quality
of license plates and
thought to use them as
the 'facades' for my
photo assemblage
series."

Janette Schuster
(above - top)

*Typewriter Key Jewelry
series*, 2005, ⅝ x 7½–15½
x ⅛"/1.6 x 19–39.4 x .3 cm.
Typewriter keys, glass
beads, wire, findings.

Janette Schuster
(above - bottom)

Take a Chance, 2003,
17"/43.2 cm.
Game pieces, glass and
wood beads, cord, paper
ephemera, ink, button.

"I have a passion for
collecting and, as a writer,
I was drawn to vintage
typewriters. When my
typewriter collection began
taking over my house, out of
self-defense I started making
jewelry from their parts."

"Vintage game pieces are
another item I have a
passion for collecting. I
gathered a few numbers with
personal meaning and used
just a small percentage of
my ever-growing collection
to make this necklace."

Stephanie Rubiano
(above)

For a Moment, 2003,
2 x 1¼"/5 x 3.2 cm.
Glass, solder, copper tape,
grosgrain ribbon, vintage
paper, pin finding.

"My glass houses pin
series came about from
my desire to preserve
ephemeral bits such as
vintage paper and ribbon
within something that
would withstand time
longer than they could.
The house shape itself
was a logical choice
because many of our
thoughts and feelings are
tightly associated with
our dwellings, which tend
to keep us safe within
their walls."

Giuseppina
"Josie" Cirincione
(above)

Ciminna, 2007,
13 x 3½ x ⅛"/33 x 8.9 x
.3 cm.
Nickel silver wire,
vintages photos,
decorative paper,
microscope slide glass,
solder, copper tape.

"The inspiration for
this piece comes from
the memories I have of
the last road trip my
family took from England
to Sicily. We would
drive to the coast of
England, take a ferry
over to Italy, drive
down to Naples, board
another ferry, and then
drive to my parents'
home town of Ciminna. My
brother is number 1 and
I am number 3."

QUILTERS HAVE LONG USED fabric, needle, and thread to preserve memories and record their personal histories. For the collage jewelry artist, the contents of the sewing box and button jar, whether our own or an ancestor's, can evoke memories and provide a means of recording them. When combined with traditional jewelry materials such as wire and findings, as well as less-traditional collage materials, the "gentle arts" take on a whole new meaning and form of adornment.

Most women of my mother's and grandmother's generations collected buttons out of necessity. As a result, just about every estate sale includes buried treasure in the form of a forgotten button box. To me, vintage buttons filling an old cookie tin seem as abundant and desirable as Spanish doubloons in a treasure chest. It can be a real test of my self-discipline to pass by a flea market stall displaying colorful button cards or jars without at least stopping to take a peek. The predrilled, beadlike quality of buttons makes them ideal

> "To me, vintage buttons filling an old cookie tin seem as abundant and desirable as Spanish doubloons in a treasure chest."

for use in jewelry. And buttons often have a sentimental connotation that makes them appealing for use in keepsake jewelry since, for every special event in your life, you were likely wearing clothing with buttons. Even if the wedding or christening gown, favorite sweater, letter jacket, or Easter blouse you couldn't quite part with is in tatters, it's probably a good source of buttons for memory jewelry.

Keepsake garments can also provide fabric for use in jewelry, along with other salvaged materials such as trim, ribbon, lace, leather, and beads. How about including clothing fasteners such as buckles, snaps, zippers, and eyelets in your next jewelry project? Also consider

incorporating sewing objects such as tape measures and thimbles and embellishing or securing collage items together with colorful cotton or metallic thread, embroidery floss, or yarn.

If you don't have sewing materials like the ones pictured on hand already, most are easy to come by. Fabric stores have a vast selection of new and reproduction vintage fabrics available, as well as sewing notions such as buttons and trim. Watch for vintage and newer fabric and notions you can recycle at antique stores, flea markets, estate sales, and thrift stores. Don't think of the items at a thrift store as old clothes and linens but as usable fabric yardage, buttons, zippers, and lace. Additionally, you can make your own custom fabric for use in jewelry by transferring family photos on fabric (see page 55).

button charm earrings

Artist: **Luann Udell**

LIKE MANY COLLAGE ARTISTS, Luann Udell is inspired by the vintage treasures she collects. These treasures led to her inspiration for this project. As she explains, "I love vintage beads and buttons, and I have drawers full of them. I first started layering them on my fiber wall hangings, and then thought, 'These would make great earrings!'"

Materials

- Two large buttons or flat beads, approximately ⁷⁄₈"/2.2 cm diameter
- Two heishi beads (disk- or flower-shaped) or small buttons, approximately ³⁄₈"/9.5 cm diameter
- Two tiny heishi beads (flower-shaped glass or metal)
- Two sterling silver head pins, at least 2"/5 cm long
- Two sterling silver French ear wires

Tools and Supplies

- Chain-nose pliers
- Wire wrapping kit

Optional

- Jump-ring pliers
- Super glue
- Two small jump rings

MAKE IT YOUR OWN

To make your own version, start with what you already have and hold dear. Salvage buttons from a sentimental article of old clothing, such as a daughter's prom gown or father's school jacket. Ask permission to raid your grandmother's button box, or watch for colorful vintage buttons and beads on your next antiquing jaunt. Recycle small beads from your own broken jewelry.

1. Gather pairs of buttons and beads. Thread the components onto a head pin from smallest to largest, starting with a tiny heishi bead, then a larger heishi bead, and finally a large button. The fronts of the button and beads should be facing the head of the pin.
2. At the back of the large button, use chain-nose pliers to bend the head pin up to the top of the button, over the top, and back down the front of the charm (see top photo at right).
3. Again using chain-nose pliers, bend the head pin back up to the top of the button (see top photo, far right) so that about ³⁄₁₆"/5 mm of the pin "hooks" back and over the button. Gently pinch the resulting hook so it sits snugly against the button. The hook holds all the beads and the button in place, keeping them from rotating on the head pin.

Tip: If you have difficulty making the hook, keep practicing and try using different pliers. Luann sometimes uses jump-ring pliers that have a little groove in the jaws to help her hold the head pin securely as she forms the hook. You can also use a tiny dot of super glue to secure each component and prevent them from rotating.

4. Bend the head pin straight up (see bottom photo, left). To begin wire wrapping the head pin, bend it at a right angle, keeping it in the same plane as the button (see bottom photo, middle). Continue following the wire wrapping instructions on page 21 to form a loop for

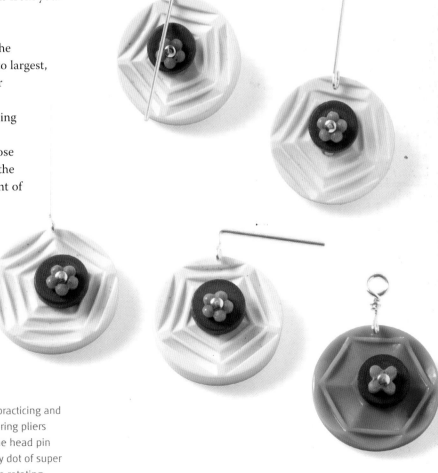

Additional Materials

- 20- or 21-gauge sterling silver wire
- Chain-nose or other pliers with insulated handles
- Small butane or other torch
- Striker
- Fine steel wool (optional)
- Safety glassses

1. Cut two pieces of sterling silver wire to the desired length plus about $1/4$"/6 mm.
2. Use pliers with insulated handles to hold the wire at one end. At the opposite end of the wire, use a small butane torch to heat about $1/2$"/1.3 cm of the wire, "stroking" the wire with the flame. The end of the wire will start to glow red and then melt to form a ball. Remove the wire from the flame and let the wire cool. If you wish, clean the blackened head pin with steel wool or using another method of your choice.

Be Careful: When using a torch, work in a well-ventilated area and use care when working with the flame. Pull back and secure long hair. Wear safety glasses and keep a fire extinguisher nearby.

hanging the charm. To ensure that the charm hangs correctly, make sure that the loop lies in the same plane as the button (see photo on page 53, bottom right).

Tip: If your loop ends up at an angle to the plane of the button, use your fingers or pliers to gently twist the loop into position. Or, use a small jump ring to attach the charm to an ear wire in step 5.

5. Repeat steps 1–4 for the second button charm to make a matching pair. Use pliers to attach the charms to ear wires.

Varying Charm Components

This technique can be adapted for a variety of components, including coconut, bone, metal, and polymer clay beads (see photo below). Bead cluster or other fancy head pins can be used. Also, small beads can be threaded onto the head pin between the hook and the wire-wrapped loop.

Handmade Head Pins Variation

If you want to use larger buttons or more components in your earrings, mass-produced head pins might not be long enough. Consider making your own custom-length head pins with ball-shaped heads (see photo above).

fabric collage choker

Artist: **Jan Bode Smiley**

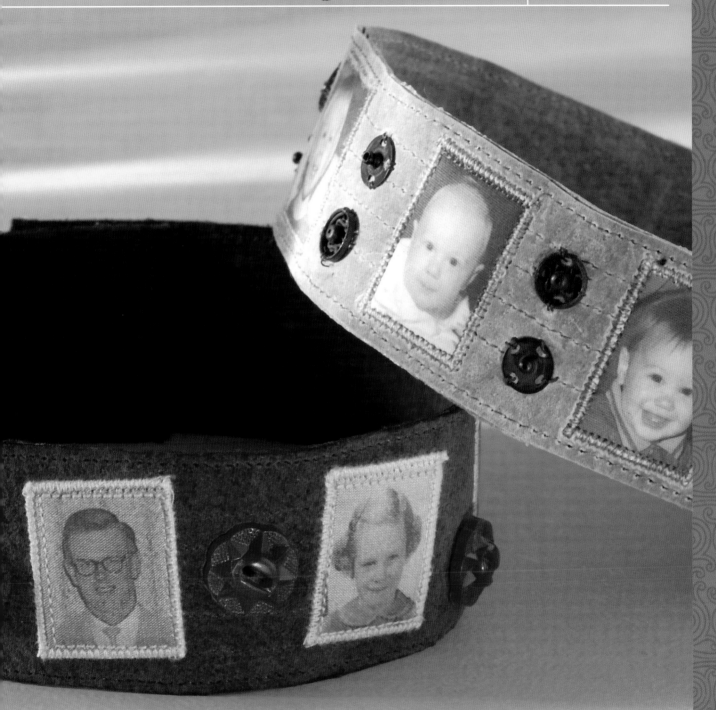

QUILT ARTIST Jan Bode Smiley is no stranger to the contents of a sewing box. She transferred treasured photos of her parents, siblings, children, and young self onto fabric and collaged them with leather, buttons, and snaps. The resulting fabric necklaces are a sentimental tribute to her multigenerational family.

Materials

- Photos
- Two strips of leather or suede, approximately 1½ x 18"/3.8 x 45.7 cm
- Sew-in computer printer fabric
- Fusible webbing
- Batting, fleece, or flannel
- Light-colored fabric
- Thread in color of your choice
- Hook-and-loop tape, approximately 1"/2.5 cm
- Embellishments such as small buttons, beads, or snaps
- Thick white glue or fabric adhesive

Tools and Supplies

- Computer with imaging software, scanner, and printer
- Printer paper
- Iron
- Ironing board
- Sewing needle
- Scissors

Optional

- Sewing machine
- Fabric marker

MAKE IT YOUR OWN

To make your own version, use an assortment of your own photos of family, friends, pets, or even vacation locales. Ask each person pictured to contribute a button or other keepsake for an embellishment. Use new leather or, as Jan did, recycle suede from a thrift store purchase or a family member's closet—just toss it in the washing machine before cutting it up. This technique can also be adapted for a bracelet, armband, or belt.

1. Choose 5 to 7 different photos for each choker. Scan them into your computer.
2. Using imaging software, crop out distracting backgrounds and adjust the color, contrast, and size of the photos as needed. Adjust the size so the height of each photo when printed is less than the height of your choker, about postage-stamp size or a maximum of 1"/2.5 cm high.
3. Print a trial run onto paper, and make adjustments until you are satisfied with the size, color, and quality of your print (see photo below, left).
4. Print the final photos onto a sheet of computer printer fabric. Follow the manufacturer's instructions for either heat setting the fabric photos or allowing them to dry for a specified time before proceeding. Do not cut out the photos yet; leave them intact on the fabric sheet.

7. Create photo charms by carefully cutting the photos apart well outside the stitch line, to avoid breaking the stitches (see photo below).

8. For textural interest, add four evenly spaced rows of machine or hand stitching along the length of one of the leather strips. Then, arrange your photo charms on the right side of that leather strip as desired. Keep in mind that any charms near the back of the choker may not be readily visible.

9. Use a spare or rejected photo charm and leather scrap to test your chosen thread color and sewing machine's tension setting. Replace the thread and adjust the tension setting as needed. Then, sew the charms to the leather strip. Pull the thread ends through to the back of the leather strip, and then knot and trim them.

Tip: Don't have a sewing machine or can't use one? Jan suggests hand stitching or using a good fabric adhesive instead of machine sewing any part of this project.

10. Arrange embellishments such as buttons, beads, or snaps between your photo charms. Sew them on by hand. Again, pull the thread ends through to the back of the leather strip, and then knot and trim them.

11. Apply a thin, even layer of glue to the wrong side of the second leather strip. Carefully lay the wrong side of the photo-collaged strip onto the glue side of the second strip, and firmly press the layers together all the way around. Let the glue dry for several minutes.

5. Make a fabric "sandwich" by stacking the following layers: a top layer of photos on the fabric sheet; a second layer of fusible webbing; a third layer of batting, fleece, or flannel; a fourth layer of fusible webbing; and a fifth (bottom) layer of light-colored fabric.

6. Following the manufacturer's instructions for the fusible webbing, use an iron to fuse together the layers of the fabric sandwich. By sewing machine or by hand, carefully stitch all around each photo near its edge (see photos above).

Be Careful: Be careful when using a hot iron. Avoid touching any part but the handle, and do not leave a hot iron unattended.

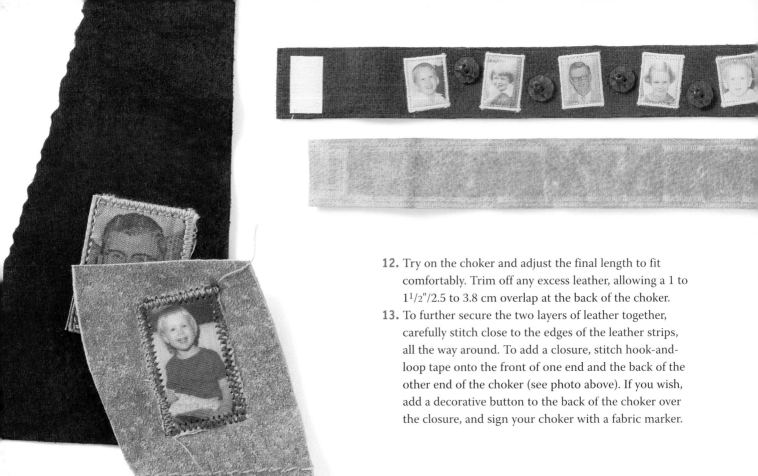

12. Try on the choker and adjust the final length to fit comfortably. Trim off any excess leather, allowing a 1 to 1¹/₂"/2.5 to 3.8 cm overlap at the back of the choker.

13. To further secure the two layers of leather together, carefully stitch close to the edges of the leather strips, all the way around. To add a closure, stitch hook-and-loop tape onto the front of one end and the back of the other end of the choker (see photo above). If you wish, add a decorative button to the back of the choker over the closure, and sign your choker with a fabric marker.

optical lens earrings

Artist: **Jannette Schuster**

I CONFESS, when my sister and I get together, we do love to shop. I made these earrings as a gift for her using silk tie fabric discovered on a shared shopping expedition, keepsake yarn, and photos of two of our unknown ancestors (who probably loved to shop, too).

Materials

- Two matching or similar optical lenses
- Two photos
- Fabric scrap for background
- Heavy gel medium, preferably matte
- Scraps of ribbon, trim, lace, or yarn
- Aluminum flashing, approximately 2½ x 4"/6.4 x 11.4 cm
- Two sterling silver French ear wires

Tools and Supplies

- Drilling kit with ¹⁄₁₆"/1.6 mm cobalt bit
- Paper collage kit
- Fabric marker
- Fabric scissors
- Glass cleaner
- Paper towel
- Small glue brush
- Utility knife with extra blades

- Awl or pencil
- Metal shears or scissors
- Mallet
- Emery board
- Fine steel wool
- Kitchen scouring pad or medium steel wool
- Bone folder
- Pliers (any with small nose)
- Photocopier (optional)

MAKE IT YOUR OWN

To make your own version, search online or at your local rubber stamp, scrapbook, or craft store for optical lenses. (Opticians use these glass lenses framed in metal to test a patient's vision, and vintage examples make great frames for collage earrings and pendants.) Gather family photos and your own keepsake scraps of fabric, ribbon, trim, lace, or yarn to make a pair of small, personal collages. You might use fabric from your Dad's tie, lace from your grandmother's wedding dress, or trim from your grandchild's christening gown.

1. Use a ¹⁄₁₆"/1.6 mm cobalt drill bit (for steel) to drill a hanging hole in the "handle" of each optical lens (shown below).
2. Choose a photo to fit within the frame of each lens (or resize the photos as needed using a photocopier). Photocopy and then use small, sharp scissors to cut the photos out.

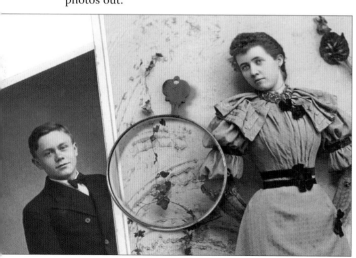

3. Choose the fabric for the background of the collage. I chose silk with a graphic pattern in a favorite color that contrasts with my chosen photos (see photo above).
4. Use heavy gel medium to adhere each photo to a piece of the fabric. Unlike other glues, heavy gel medium won't be absorbed by the fabric, which could affect its color.
5. To each collage, add accent fibers such as yarn, ribbon, lace, or trim. Use gel medium to tack the fibers in spots to the background fabric (see photo on page 61, top). Let the gel medium dry.
6. Position an optical lens over each fabric collage, and trace around the outside of the lens onto the collage with a fabric marker. Using sharp fabric scissors, cut out each collage on or just outside the tracing line.

(Remember that it is better to have a bit too much fabric, which can be trimmed later, rather than too little.) Clean the lenses as needed.

7. Working quickly, use a small brush to apply a thin line of heavy gel medium on the underside of the metal rim of one optical lens and around the outside of one collage, just inside the traced line. Immediately press the lens onto the collage to adhere them. Quickly brush more gel medium all around the outer edge of the collage and wrap the fabric around the metal rim of the lens. Repeat this step for the second collage and lens, and let the gel medium dry.

8. Put a sharp new blade in a utility knife and use it to trim off any excess fabric adhered to the front rim of each lens. As you cut on the metal rim, the blade will quickly become dull, so change it as needed to keep your blade sharp.

9. Make a pronged backing piece for each lens to protect the fabric collage. Place each lens faceup on a sheet of aluminum flashing. Use an awl or pencil (not a marker, which might bleed into the fabric) to trace around each lens onto the flashing. Don't trace the lens "handle." Remove each lens and on each tracing draw four prongs, equidistant around the tracing (like compass

points) and about $1/4"/6$ mm in length or shorter. Use scissors or metal shears to cut out the aluminum (see photo below). If needed, flatten the metal with a mallet and finish the edges with an emery board and fine steel wool. Use a kitchen scouring pad or medium steel wool to give the aluminum a matte finish.

10. Position each backing piece behind a lens, and attach it by bending the prongs around the front of the lens using your fingers and a bone folder. Do not bend and open the prongs repeatedly, or you will overwork the metal and the prongs may break off. Use pliers to attach the charms to ear wires.

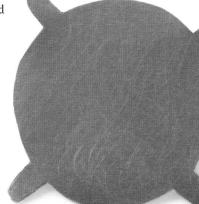

gallery

Janette Schuster
(left)

Dreams of Flight,
2003, 2 x 6½"/5 x 15.2 cm.
Glass beads and button;
ultrasuede; polymer clay,
glass, and plastic
cabochons; wood game
piece; paper; brass
findings; bone; thread.

"Family keepsakes,
including my
grandmother's button, my
grandfather's photo, and
my sister's Alaskan
vacation souvenir, as
well as my childhood
dreams of flying
inspired this colorful
embroidered bracelet."

Susan Skinner
(left)

Circle Brooch, 2003,
3½"/8.2 cm diameter.
Sterling silver, vintage
bakelite buttons.

"Each of these button
pieces is like a 'memory'
piece. Not only do I have
the memory of how I
acquired these buttons—
gifts from friends,
family heirlooms, flea
market finds—I also try
to imagine the life of
these buttons and other
found objects. Whose
clothing were they on 50
or 100 years ago? Where
have these buttons
traveled and what have
they seen?"

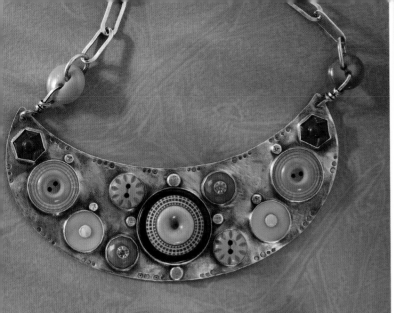

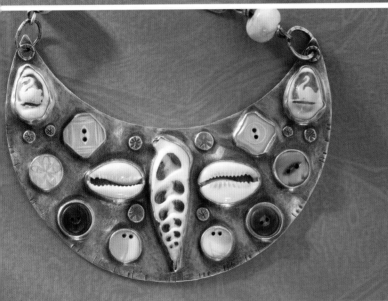

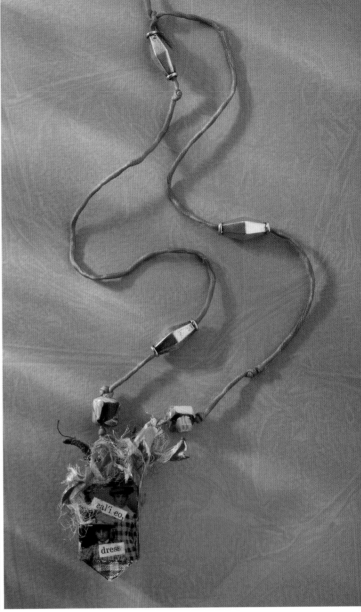

Susan Skinner
(above - top)

Button Crescent Neckpiece, 2003, 2½ x 5"/6.4 x 12.7 cm (14½"/36.8 cm long with chain).
Sterling silver, vintage bakelite, and plastic buttons.

Susan Skinner
(above - bottom)

Large Crescent Neckpiece, 2003, 3¼ x 4½"/8.2 x 11.4 cm (14"/35.6 cm long with chain).
Sterling silver, antique buttons, shells.

Lou McCulloch
(above)

Homespun Girls, 2007, 16 x 1 x ¾"/40.6 x 2.5 x 1.9 cm.
Wood block, tintypes, vintage fabric, text, beads, rolled ribbon, brass screw eye.

"My inspiration for this necklace was my love of old calico fabric, including the fabric in the dresses pictured in the tintypes and the scraps of fabric collaged onto wood."

THEY SAY SCENT EVOKES memories, but for most of us, a picture really does conjure up a thousand words, or remembrances. The invention of the camera and its product, the photograph, changed how we make art and how we record and recall the past. Photographs are moments in time captured; they are memories preserved. Thus, photographs would seem to be the quintessential memory jewelry material.

Some of my favorite photographs to use in jewelry include vintage black-and-white or sepia-toned photos of my ancestors. I also love tintypes, which are photos printed on a thin sheet of metal. These durable, Victorian-era images can be cut and riveted just like other sheet metals.

Even if you don't have a vast collection of old family photos, there are many ways you can use photos and other imagery to create a uniquely personal picture of the past. Take and use modern photos of your family, friends, and experiences. Digital photography and computer imaging software make personal photography immediate and accessible. Using computer imaging, you can even give modern color photos a vintage sepia-toned appearance.

To find forgotten photos, you might not need to look any further than your family photo album. Or do a little digging: check your attic and basement, the photo boxes in the back of your closet, the shoeboxes under the bed, or the collection in the hope chest. Ask family members and friends for vintage or new family photos for use in collage jewelry. Rather than use the originals, you may wish to scan and print out or photocopy them. Some artists use only reproductions of personal photos; others prefer to use only original, impersonal photos.

> "Photographs are moments in time captured; they are memories preserved."

Consider using other kinds of photographically reproduced imagery, too, such as vintage postcards, advertising images, engravings, and postage stamps. You might also use your own paints or drawings, or reproductions of these original works of art, in your collage jewelry.

I am lucky enough to have at least one photo of each of my great grandparents. Admittedly, they aren't all good photos, so I often honor my photo-challenged ancestors by designating photo "stand-ins." I search for and purchase what I call "anonymous ancestors"—photos of someone else's unidentified family members that have found their way into the commercial collective; in other words, unwanted portrait photos that are up for grabs at yard sales, antique stores, online auctions, and flea markets. These venues are good sources of all sorts of potential collage jewelry imagery.

Keep in mind that you don't have to use a photograph exactly as you found it. Consider enhancing or altering it with computer imaging software or art materials such as colored pencils, paint, metal leaf, or glitter.

Before using a "found" photo or other image—one that you did not take or create yourself—in your own piece of jewelry that may be published or sold, remember to always consider copyright issues. In many cases, using someone else's art is illegal. When in doubt, don't use someone else's imagery before consulting an attorney who is an expert on copyright law.

vintage slide binder necklace | Artist: **Janette Schuster**

I LOVE TO TRAVEL and gather souvenirs of my adventures. To commemorate a trip to the Big Apple to view its architectural wonders, I made this two-sided necklace using vintage photos and postcards. I also used a photographic found object called a slide binder—a vintage steel and glass contraption once used to create a slide for a slide projector.

Materials

- Metal slide binder, approximately 2¾ x 2¾"/6.9 x 6.9 cm or 2 x 2"/5 x 5 cm
- Travel-themed images, such as vintage or new photos and postcards
- 20- or 22-gauge silver coated copper wire, approximately 7"/17.8 cm
- Small souvenir(s) or charm
- Two large silver jump rings, approximately ¼"/6 mm
- One or two smaller silver jump rings
- Two pieces silver chain, approximately 10"/25.4 cm each
- Closure, such as lobster clasp and spring ring

Tools and Supplies

- Glass or general-purpose cleaner
- Paper towels
- Paper collage kit
- Photocopier or computer with imaging software, scanner, and printer
- Ultrafine-point black permanent marker
- Flat-nose pliers
- Masking tape
- Drilling kit with ¹⁄₁₆"/1.5 mm cobalt bit
- Ruler
- Wire wrapping kit

Optional

- Acrylic paint in color of your choice
- Small paintbrush
- Alphabet rubber stamps
- Black die ink
- Kitchen scouring pad
- Patina kit with pewter black patina solution
- Wax polish
- Industrial adhesive

MAKE IT YOUR OWN

To make a personalized version, use your own travel-themed photos and souvenirs to commemorate a favorite vacation. Consider gathering kitschy or humorous postcards or advertising images from the 1930s and '40s to make your own funky collages. Or create your own images of the dream trip to Paris or Bora Bora that you still hope to take some day. To find vintage slide binders, check your parents' or grandparents' attic, camera collector club shows, flea markets, and online auctions.

1. Slide binders come in cardboard, plastic, and metal and in two basic sizes (see photo below). I used one of the larger size binders made of two steel frames with two glass slides. If necessary, disassemble the binder according to the manufacturer's instructions (this often involves placing one edge of the binder on a table and lightly pressing down on the glass to uncouple the two metal frames). Clean the metal frames inside and out. Clean the glass slides.

2. Plan and make two collages following the instructions for paper collage on page 24, and use imaging software

or a photocopier to reduce the collages as needed to fit within the binder's frames. For the front of the necklace, I collaged a large vintage photo of a man with images of buildings from vintage postcards, and I reduced the collage by 75 percent using a photocopier. I added color to the background using acrylic paint and used rubber stamps to add the abbreviation "NYC." For the back of the necklace, I chose a vintage souvenir postcard image of a favorite building and reduced it by 25 percent using a photocopier (see photo above).

Tip: Instead of starting with small images that fit inside the binder frames, collage oversized images and then reduce them to fit. Doing so can minimize flaws and intensify colors, giving faded vintage images a bit more vibrancy and impact. Doing so also minimizes the thickness of the collaged layers inside the slide binder, which was originally designed to hold only a single thin photo transparency without breaking.

3. Trim both collages as needed to fit within the binder's frames and between the glass slides. Use a dab of paper adhesive to adhere the two collages back-to-back. Let the adhesive dry.

4. Reassemble the two metal frames only, without the glass slides. The front of the binder has a brand name stamped on it, and the back has rectangular holes. Flip the binder to the back and orient it so the edges with two holes become the top and bottom of the binder. Insert the point of an ultrafine-point marker into each of the top two holes, centered in each hole, and mark the position for two drill holes on the inside top of the front frame. Using flat-nose pliers (with its jaws wrapped in masking tape to prevent damage to the frame), disassemble the two metal frames. Drill the two marked holes in the front frame using a $^1/_{16}$"/1.5 mm cobalt bit. (Don't punch the holes, since the punch may distort the frame.)

5. With the inside of the back frame facing up, use a ruler to find the center of the bottom edge. Mark the center point against the bottom edge, and drill a hole at the mark (see photo below). Reassemble the two metal frames. Insert the drill bit in the hole you just drilled in the back frame, and drill a matching hole through the front frame. Disassemble the frames.

6. Finish the metal frames as you prefer. You can leave the steel as you found it, give it a brushed finish by rubbing it with a kitchen scouring pad, or treat it with a patina solution. I used a light application of pewter black patina solution to knock down the shine of the steel. You might also want to use the patina solution on any findings (closure, jump rings, chain, charms, wire) and seal the finish with a wax polish.

7. Clean the glass slides again and sandwich the two-sided collage between the slides. Carefully assemble the binder according to the manufacturer's instructions (this often involves making sure the glass slides rest

inside the metal prongs on the bottom frame and using your finger to hold the glass and bottom frame securely to the table as you align and press on the top frame). Make sure the collage images are oriented so the last hole you drilled is at the base of the slide binder.

8. Choose a souvenir or charm to hang from the slide binder. I made my charm by adhering a toy compass to a subway token using industrial adhesive, then drilling a hole in the token. Use wire wrapping (as described on page 21) to hang the charm from the binder (see photo above).

9. Use large jump rings to attach each section of chain to the top of the slide binder. Use small jump rings to attach each part of the closure to the other ends of the chain.

angel necklace

Artist: **Janette Schuster**

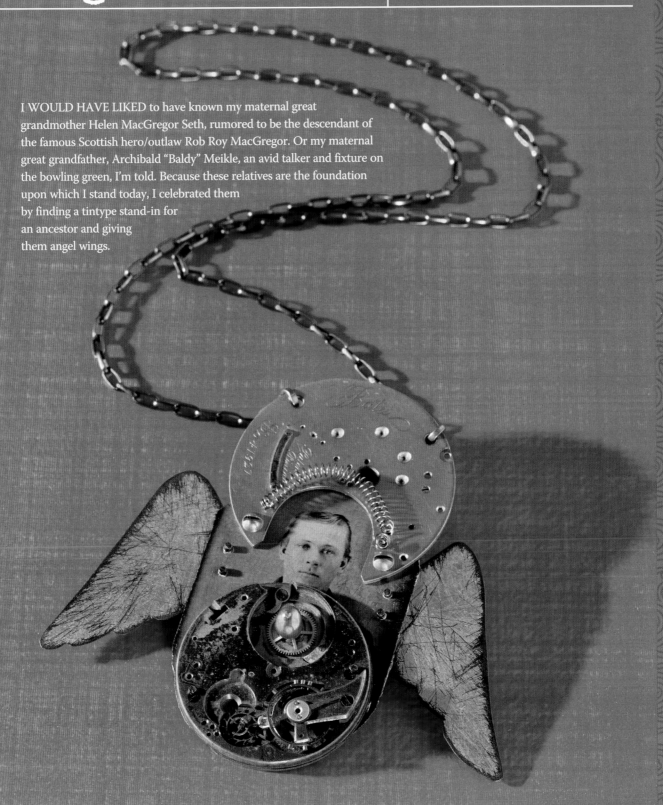

I WOULD HAVE LIKED to have known my maternal great grandmother Helen MacGregor Seth, rumored to be the descendant of the famous Scottish hero/outlaw Rob Roy MacGregor. Or my maternal great grandfather, Archibald "Baldy" Meikle, an avid talker and fixture on the bowling green, I'm told. Because these relatives are the foundation upon which I stand today, I celebrated them by finding a tintype stand-in for an ancestor and giving them angel wings.

Materials

- Tintype
- Acrylic gloss medium
- Cookie tin or other thin sheet metal
- Found objects and keepsakes such as watch parts, gears, springs, and pearl beads
- Rivets such as #20 brass escutcheon pins and #19 steel wire brads
- 26-gauge red or yellow brass sheet
- Screws and matching nuts, such as #2-56 x ¼"/6 mm brass pan-head machine
- Brass chain, approximately 17"/43.2 cm
- Two brass jump rings
- Two brass lobster clasps

Tools and Supplies

- Paintbrush
- Leather gloves
- Safety glasses
- Can opener
- Metal shears
- Paper or thin cardboard
- Pencil
- Paper scissors
- Ultrafine-point black permanent marker
- Metal scissors
- Emery board
- Finishing kit
- Awl
- Soft cloth
- Patina kit with gun blue patina solution
- Drilling kit with ⁵⁄₆₄"/2 mm, #59, and #61 drill bits
- Pin vise
- Water
- Riveting kit
- Small clamp
- Mallet
- Wire cutters
- Sawing kit (optional)

MAKE IT YOUR OWN

To make your own version, honor one of your relatives—perhaps a grandparent or great grandparent—who you never got the chance to know. If you don't have or prefer not to use your own family tintype, find a tintype stand-in at an antique shop or flea market. Include in your necklace other materials with sentimental value, like Mom's old cookie tin and Grandpa's pocket watch parts. This technique can also be adapted for a pin.

1. Choose a tintype portrait and seal the surface with several coats of gloss medium. Let the medium dry between coats.

2. Every angel needs its wings, so choose thin sheet metal from which to cut the wings for your pendant. Cookie and other food tins are a good source of colorful sheet metal (see photo, left). Cut tins into sheets using a can opener and metal shears.

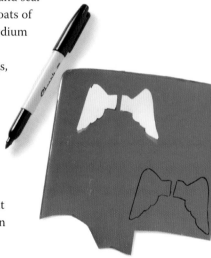

Be Careful: Use caution when handling cut sheet metal; the edges can be extremely sharp. Wear leather gloves and eye protection.

3. Sketch a simple pair of wings, either similar to those pictured above or of your own design. Include an extra segment at the shoulder of each wing for attaching the wing to the tintype. (To get the proportions right for your tintype, you may need to enlarge or reduce your sketch using a photocopier.) Cut out the wings and use a marker to trace them onto the sheet metal. Cut out the wings using sharp scissors or shears.

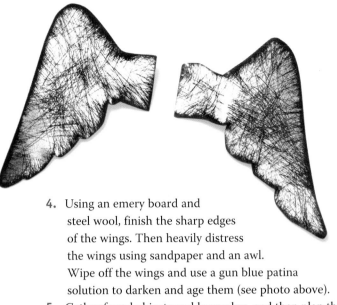

4. Using an emery board and steel wool, finish the sharp edges of the wings. Then heavily distress the wings using sandpaper and an awl. Wipe off the wings and use a gun blue patina solution to darken and age them (see photo above).

5. Gather found objects and keepsakes, and then plan the collage design (see photo below). I used two vintage brass pocket watch "guts" for the body and halo of my angel. As you audition objects for use in your collage, keep the scale of your piece in mind and discard parts that are so small they get lost or so large they throw the piece out of balance. Help new, shiny objects blend in by aging them with patina solution. Once you plan your design, decide on the order and method for attaching the collage parts using the following steps as a guide. The size of the rivets and screws you use may vary depending on existing holes in your watch parts and found object embellishments. (If you don't have exiting holes, you will need to drill some.)

Tip: Instead of using vintage found objects, you can create halos, hats, clothes, and other embellishments for your tintype person using cookie tins in the same manner that you created wings. You can also use new pocket watch "guts" and age them with patina solution.

6. To attach a pearl bead, you might need to first ream, or enlarge, the bead's hole. Using a #61 drill bit in a pin vise, place the bit in the existing hole and carefully turn the vise by hand. Periodically dip the bit in water to lubricate it and prevent the pearl from breaking. Once reamed, use a #20 brass escutcheon pin to rivet the pearl and watch gear below it to the pocket watch part (see photo page 72, left: I took advantage of an existing hole in the watch part body, so I did not need to drill a hole for the rivet). Set the rivet slowly and carefully, so as not to the shatter the pearl.

7. In the same manner, attach any other embellishments you like to the watch parts. I used existing holes in the watch part halo and riveted a found spring to it using two #20 brass escutcheon pins.

8. Use scissors to trim the tintype to the desired size or shape. Use a small file and steel wool to finish any sharp edges. Next, prepare a backing layer to support the thin tintype. With a marker, trace the tintype on 26-gauge brass sheet and cut out the shape just inside the tracing line with shears or a saw. File the backing layer so it will not be visible behind the tintype when viewed from the front of the piece. Then, use steel wool to give it a smooth finish. If you wish, sign the backing at this time by stamping your name or initials in the metal.

9. Mark four holes on the tintype for attaching the wings with rivets. Gently dimple and drill the holes using a #59 drill bit. Be sure to clamp near the dimple location, because the thin metal deforms easily during drilling. If it does become deformed, use a mallet to flatten it again

as needed. Drill four coordinating holes in the wings and attach them to the tintype using #19 steel wire brads as rivets.

10. Position the watch part halo over the tintype and the brass backing layer beneath the tintype. Using two existing holes in the watch part halo as a template, drill coordinating holes in the tintype and backing layer. I used a $^5/_{64}$"/2 mm bit and then two #2-56 × $^1/_4$"/6 mm brass pan-head machine screws and nuts to attach the three layers.

Tip: If the shiny surfaces of new rivets and screws stand out against vintage found objects, consider aging them with patina solution before setting them. Or, after setting them, dip a cotton swab in patina solution and touch it to the head of each rivet or screw, then wipe with a slightly wet cloth to arrest the patination.

11. Repeat step 10 for the watch part body. This time, use two or three existing holes and a #59 drill bit. Instead of screwing the three layers together, rivet them using #19 steel wire brads.

12. Cut the chain to the desired length. Attach a jump ring to each end of the chain, and use the jump rings to attach lobster clasps to the chain. Clip the clasps to existing holes in the watch part halo.

Tip: When hanging a pendant, choose a chain that complements the piece but doesn't overpower it. For this necklace, I chose a simple vintage brass watch chain that doesn't distract you from the main focus of the piece, which is the gold-toned pendant.

photo transfer pin

Artist: **Stephanie Jones Rubiano**

SINCE HAVING A DAUGHTER of her own, jewelry artist Stephanie Rubiano often includes vintage photos of children in her work. Once she found a way to transfer those photos onto metal, a new world of collage photo pins opened up for her. She adds, "The metal [photo] base lends itself to the cold connection attachment of all sorts of accessories made from vintage tins. It is so much fun to make a new, funky wardrobe for my uptight Victorian people!"

Materials

- Photo of family member
- Transfer paper for inkjet printers
- 24-gauge nickel silver sheet
- Decorative vintage tin
- Metal tape measure
- 00-90 pan-head bolts and nuts
- Pin back

Tools and Supplies

- Computer with imaging software, scanner, and inkjet printer
- Metal shears
- Sawing kit
- Finishing kit
- Can opener
- Metal scissors
- Drilling kit with #55 drill bit
- Flush cutter
- Super glue
- Two-part jeweler's epoxy

MAKE IT YOUR OWN

To make your own version, use a photo of a family member, such as your child or your own uptight Victorian ancestor. To clothe your family member, use an old decorative tin you have on hand or pick one up at your local antique or thrift shop.

1. Chose a photo of a family member. Scan the photo into your computer, and then use imaging software to adjust the size and alter the photo as desired. Using your inkjet printer, print a color version of the photo onto transfer paper (see photo below).
2. Use metal shears to cut a piece of nickel silver sheet slightly larger than the photo you printed out (as shown below). Follow the manufacturer's instructions to apply the photo transfer decal to the nickel silver.
3. Use a jeweler's saw to cut out the metal photo. Finish the edges so they are smooth, taking care not to damage the transfer.

4. Follow the instructions and caution on page 70 to cut up your decorative vintage tin into sheets. Using metal shears or scissors, cut out accessories—such as a crown, hat, skirt, or shirt— from the tin sheets (see photo, top right). Cut a section of metal tape measure to the desired length. Finish any sharp edges on the cut metal pieces.

Tip: When choosing sheet metal for accessories, Stephanie looks for vintage tins with unusual patterns and colors or interesting weathered surfaces.

5. Using a #55 bit, drill holes in the accessories and coordinating holes in the metal photo (see photo, right). Using miniature bolts and nuts, attach the accessories to the metal photo (see photo below). If the bolt shafts are too long, use a flush cutter to crop the excess. Add a drop of super glue to secure each nut.
6. Adhere a pin back to the back of the piece using two-part jeweler's epoxy, and let the epoxy dry.

patinated copper pendant

Artist: **Linda O'Brien**

LINDA O'BRIEN'S PENDANT entitled *Dress Rehearsal* was inspired by a song about first love, but it is really a tribute to the kind of enduring love we all hope to experience. She says, "Once it was finished, I found that I couldn't part with [this piece], as it reminds me of the magical connection that my husband Opie and I share and have always felt since the first moment we met in 1984. We just knew we were destined to be together." We should all be so fortunate!

Materials

- 22-gauge copper sheet, approximately 3 x 2"/7.6 x 5 cm
- Polishing wax or acrylic matte medium
- Photo
- Mica
- Four $1/16$"/1.5 mm long silver eyelets
- One $1/8$"/3 mm short copper eyelet
- Three copper jump rings, approximately $3/16$"/5 mm
- Copper chain
- Copper or sterling silver closure
- Small watch gear (optional)

Tools and Supplies

- Ultrafine-point black permanent marker
- Metal shears
- Drilling kit with $1/16$"/1.5 mm and $1/8$"/3 mm drill bits
- Nibbling shears
- Finishing kit
- Special patina kit, including:
  - Rubber gloves
  - Safety glasses
  - Small plastic container
  - One teaspoon borax detergent
  - Water
  - Disposable spoon
  - Bowl (for water bath)
- Heat-resistant soldering surface
- Torch (such as propane)
- Tweezers or pliers
- Two plastic containers that fit one inside the other, with a lid for the larger container
- Ammonia
- Metal screen or hardware cloth
- Eyelet setter
- Hammer
- Bench block
- Pliers
- $1/16$"/1.5 mm metal punch (optional)
- $1/8$"/3 mm metal punch (optional)
- Photocopier (optional)

MAKE IT YOUR OWN

To make your own version, use a photo of yourself and someone you love—perhaps your spouse, child, or parent. Or, use a photo that represents what enduring love means to you.

1. Use a marker to draw a house shape on your copper sheet, about 2"/5 cm high × 1$1/2$"/3.8 cm wide. Cut out the shape with metal shears (see photo, top right).

2. Inside the house shape, draw a rectangular window about 1"/2.5 cm high × $3/4$"/1.9 cm wide. Drill or punch a hole in the center of the window just large enough to insert the head of the nibbling shears (see photo, center right). To use the tool, squeeze the handle, release it, and repeat the process until you have nibbled away the window. (Alternatively, you can use a jeweler's saw to cut out the window.)

3. Using a $1/16$"/1.5 mm bit, drill (or punch) two holes above and two holes below the corner of each window. Using a $1/8$"/3 mm bit, drill (or punch) a hole near the peak of the house.

4. Use metal shears to cut a rectangular backing piece from the copper sheet. The piece should be large enough to cover the window and the four $1/16$"/1.5 mm holes (see photo, bottom right). Finish the edges of the house and rectangle, and clean their outer surfaces with fine steel wool.

5. Linda used a multistage process to give the two copper pieces a colorful patinated finish. In a small plastic

container, make a slurry by mixing borax detergent and a few drops of water. Use a spoon to coat the outside of both copper pieces with the slurry, and then let them sit for several minutes. With the spoon, wipe off almost all of the borax so that you leave the surface just a little grainy. Place the copper pieces on a heat-resistant surface. Using a torch, heat the copper slowly by moving the flame in a circular motion until the copper glows orange. Immediately quench the copper pieces in a water bath. The copper should now have a reddish patina (see photo page 77, bottom left).

Be Careful:

Remember to follow the safety precautions for working with patina solutions (page 22) and using a torch (page 54).

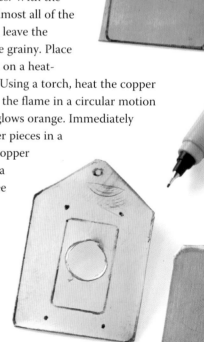

mica and trim the photo sandwich so it is a little larger than your window.

8. Stack the photo sandwich on the copper rectangle and the house on top of the photo sandwich. Using a $1/16$"/1.5 mm bit and the holes in the copper house as a template, drill (or punch) four coordinating holes through the bottom two layers. Insert and set a silver eyelet ($1/16$"/1.5 mm) in each hole. If you wish, thread a watch gear (with a $1/16$"/1.5 mm hole) onto one of the eyelets before setting it. Then, set a copper eyelet ($1/8$"/3 mm) in the hole at the peak (see photo below).

9. Using jump rings, attach each part of the closure to either end of the chain. Attach the pendant to the chain with a jump ring.

6. Into another small plastic container, pour about $1/2$ cup/ 120 ml of ammonia. Cut a piece of metal screen to fit and then place it on top of the container. Place the container and screen inside another larger container. Set the copper pieces on the screen (well above the ammonia), and then put a lid on the larger container. Let the copper pieces sit overnight. Remove them, rinse them very quickly in water, and let them air dry. The copper should now have a red and blue-green patina. Seal the pieces with wax or several thin coats of matte medium.

7. Choose a photograph and, if needed, use a photocopier to adjust its size to fit within the window (see photo, above). Sandwich the photo between two thin sheets of

bottle head pin

Artist: **Beth Piver**

WANT TO INJECT A LITTLE HUMOR into some staid photos in your family album? Then Beth Piver's Bottle Head Pin is the project for you. Beth's light-hearted piece reflects her fascination with the colorful characters of circuses and sideshows. She included some of her favorite things—wheels, springs, and spinning pieces—to give the pin movement.

Materials

- ⁵⁄₃₂"/4 mm brass square tubing
- ⅛"/3 mm copper round tubing
- 22-gauge copper sheet
- 22-gauge nickel silver sheet
- 22-gauge patterned or etched brass sheet
- 20-gauge sterling silver wire, approximately 16"/40 cm
- Photo of a face
- Small glass bottle with opening ⁷⁄₃₂"/5.5 mm to ¼"/6 mm in diameter (to fit over ⁵⁄₃₂"/4 mm brass square tubing)
- Two hand-shaped stampings, one silver, one copper (optional)
- Two tiny hinges
- Two star-shaped metal stampings
- Rivets, such as #19 steel wire brads
- Pin back
- One 0-80 x ¾"/1.9 cm pan-head screw
- One #2-56 hex nut
- Eight 0-80 x ½"/1.3 cm pan- or hex-head screws
- Nine 0-80 hex nuts
- Spinner or similar jewelry finding
- Cone-shaped spinner holder or 0-80 hex nut
- Domed perforated disk or similar jewelry finding
- Two wheels
- Two wheel holders or 0-80 hex nuts

Tools and Supplies

- Sawing kit
- Ultrafine-point black permanent marker
- Paper scissors
- Rubber cement
- Finishing kit
- Wire cutter
- Photocopier or computer with imaging software, scanner, and printer
- Drilling kit with ¹⁄₁₆"/1.5 mm and #59 drill bits
- Small-nose pliers
- Miniature nut driver (or small screwdriver and small-nose pliers)
- Epoxy or super glue
- Flush cutter
- Heat-resistant soldering surface (optional)
- Torch (such as propane) (optional)

MAKE IT YOUR OWN

To make your own version, find a seriously stodgy photo in your family album, or purchase a suitable "anonymous ancestor" at an online auction or flea market. Or use a photo of yourself and have a good laugh at your own expense.

1. Gather and prepare all the materials. Use a jeweler's saw to cut out all the body pieces from the sheet metal and metal tubes. From the brass square tubing, cut the following: left hip 1"/2.5 cm, right hip (for shorter leg) 1³⁄₁₆"/3 cm, neck 1¹⁄₂"/3.8 cm (if needed, adjust the neck length to fit your bottle), and two ankles at ⁵⁄₁₆"/8 mm each. From the copper round tubing, cut two legs at 2¹⁵⁄₁₆"/2.4 cm each. Use a marker to sketch a right hand on the copper sheet and a left hand on the nickel silver, and then cut them out. (Alternatively, you can use two hand-shaped stampings.)

2. Photocopy the templates at right for the front and back bodies. Roughly cut them out and use rubber cement to adhere the front template to the patterned brass sheet and the back template to the nickel silver sheet. Let the rubber cement dry.

Tip: Beth has brass sheet custom etched for her, but you can also etch brass yourself using the instructions on page 42–43 or purchase brass sheet that is already impressed with a pattern.

3. Use a jeweler's saw to cut out the front and back bodies. Finish all the metal pieces until smooth, and use coarse sandpaper or steel wool to add a brushed texture if desired. If you want to add color to the metals, place the front body and the copper hand on a heat-resistant surface and heat them with a torch. Let them cool before handling.

4. Wrap silver wire around both copper leg pieces to form loosely spread spring coils, about $1^{1}/4$"/3.1 cm on the right leg and $1^{1}/2$"/3.8 cm on the left leg (see photo above). Trim the wire ends with a wire cutter.

5. Choose a photo of a face. Manipulate and stretch it using a photocopier or, as Beth did, using a scanner, imaging software, and a printer. Tear the photo to size, roll it slightly, and slip it into the glass bottle upside down (see photo above, right).

6. Insert the ends of each copper leg all the way inside a brass square tube hip and ankle. Using a $1/16$"/1.5 mm bit, drill a hole in the center of each ankle (for attaching the wheeled feet). Sandwich the legs between the front and back body pieces, using the photo of the finished piece as a positioning guide. In preparation for attaching the legs later, drill two holes for each leg through all the layers.

7. Sandwich the brass square tube neck between the front and back body pieces. Drill one hole through all the layers, centering the hole in the middle of the front body (for attaching the spinner). Position the copper hand on one of the hinges, and drill a hole through the hand and hinge. Do the same for the nickel silver hand and second hinge. While holding the stars with pliers, drill a hole through the middle of each star.

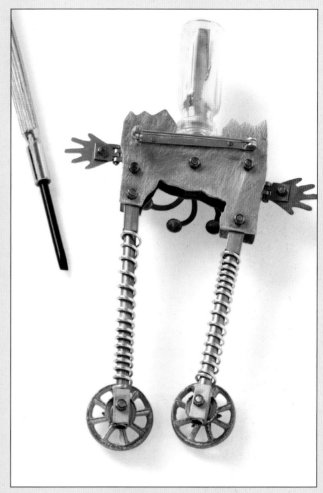

8. Position the hinges on the back side of the front body piece. Using a #59 bit, drill two holes through each hinge and the front body. Next, rivet the hinges on the front body piece using steel wire brads or rivets of your choice. Similarly, position the pin back on the back side of the back body piece, and drill two holes through the pin back and back body. Then rivet the pin back on the back body.

9. Onto the ³/₄"/1.9 cm screw, thread the #2-56 nut, spinner, spinner holder, and domed disk. Then continue threading the front body (at the center hole), neck, and back body. To attach each leg, take a ¹/₂"/1.3 cm screw and thread the front body, hip, and back body (do this twice for each leg). To assemble each wheeled foot, take a ¹/₂"/1.3 cm screw and thread the star, wheel, wheel holder, and ankle. For each hand, thread a ¹/₂"/1.3 cm screw through a hand and a hinge (see photo above).

Tip: The purpose of the spinner holder, domed disk, and wheel holders are to elevate the spinner and wheels so they can turn freely. I you don't have these parts, try substituting other found objects that could serve the same purpose, such as nuts, washers, and beads.

10. Attach nuts to all the screws and tighten them using a miniature nut driver (or small screwdriver and small-nose pliers). Remember not to tighten the nuts so much that the spinner and wheels won't spin. Add a drop of glue to each nut and let the glue dry. If the screw shafts are too long, use a flush cutter to crop the excess. Slide the bottle head onto the neck (see photo above). If you wish, use glue to secure the bottle.

Be Careful: When using epoxy or super glue, work in a well-ventilated area.

lover's eyes ring

Artist: **Janette Schuster**

JEWELRY OF THE PAST provides inspiration for many jewelry artists, including myself. This ring was inspired by a fashion trend of the 18th and 19th centuries—one of wearing jewelry set with a miniature portrait of a single eye. Referred to as "lover's eyes," these intimate love tokens often symbolized a secret love. My modern version includes an unconventional ring band and a "stone" made from a photo of a loved one's eyes transferred onto wood.

Materials

- Craft hardwood, approximately $1/4"/6$ mm thick
- Aluminum yardstick or other thick sheet metal, or square wire such as copper or sterling silver
- Facial photo
- Several black-and-white photocopies of the facial photo
- Acrylic paint in color of your choice
- Antiquing medium in brown
- Varnish or acrylic medium
- Four #20 x $1/4"/6$ mm copper brads

Tools and Supplies

- Small craft miter box
- Small craft handsaw
- Tape measure
- Metal shears
- Ultrafine-point black permanent marker
- Sawing kit
- Finishing kit
- Finger gauge
- Ring mandrel
- Mallet
- Drilling kit with #62 and #71 drill bits

- Paper scissors
- Scrap wood
- Masking tape
- Wood-burning tool with transfer point
- Heat-resistant transfer surface, such as masonite or ceramic tile
- Double-sided tape
- Small paintbrush
- Soft cloth
- Bench pin, vise, or clamp (optional)

MAKE IT YOUR OWN

To make your own version, use a modern or vintage facial photo of your loved one's eyes. Use a ruler or yardstick you have hanging around the house, or purchase one at your local home improvement store.

1. For the "stone" of the ring, use a small miter box and handsaw to cut a small rectangular block from hardwood. To determine the length of the block, measure the width of the wearer's finger and use that dimension. For the block's width, use about $1/2"/1.3$ cm, or larger if you prefer. For my version I cut a block approximately $7/8"/2.2$ cm long × $7/16"/1.1$ cm wide × $1/4"/6$ mm thick from a small wood cross purchased at my local craft store. Sand the wood smooth.

2. Choose metal for the ring band. I used an aluminum yardstick for its funky numbers and marked

increments, but you can also use copper or sterling silver. To determine the length of yardstick to cut, use a tape measure to roughly measure the circumference of the wearer's finger and add $1/2"/1.3$ cm. Use metal shears (or a jeweler's saw) to cut a section of the yardstick to at least this length.

3. With a permanent marker, mark the yardstick to the desired band width along one finished edge of the yardstick. Your ring band should be the same width as your wood block (I used $7/16"/1.1$ cm). Cut along the marked line with a jeweler's saw. Finish the cut edge to mimic the finished edge.

4. Use a finger gauge to determine the wearer's ring size (see photo page 83, top). Then use the gauge to find a mandrel of the same size. Objects such as large drill bits, pipes, broom handles, and dowels can be put to use as ring mandrels, or you can use a jeweler's ring mandrel.

5. Using your fingers, start to bend the yardstick band around the mandrel to form a "U" shape. (While shaping the band, you may find it easier to hold the mandrel against a bench pin, secure it in a vise, or clamp it to the workbench.) Then, use a mallet to further shape the ring into a U around the mandrel. Have the wearer try on the band, and insert the wood block into the top of the U until it is positioned for a comfortable fit above the finger. Mark the position of the top of the block on the band for cutting. Use a jeweler's saw to cut each end of the band and finish the cut edges.

6. Prepare to transfer an image onto the wood block. Choose a facial photo and, using a black-and-white toner copier, adjust the contrast and resize it as needed so that only the eyes fit on the top surface of the wood block. Make several copies. Trim your copies so they are about $1/4$"/6 mm larger on all sides than the top surface of the wood block. Place a copy face down on a piece of scrap wood you sanded smooth, and tape down one edge of the copy. Follow the manufacturer's instructions for using the wood-burning tool for transferring images to test your photo size and transfer technique on the scrap wood. If needed, resize your photo and practice your technique until you are satisfied with the results (see photo, right). Be sure to only briefly heat the back of the copy and keep the heated transfer tip of the tool moving on the paper. Don't overheat the paper. If the tool scorches the wood, unplug the tool and let it cool down a bit before trying again. Immediately peel the paper off the wood; don't let it cool on the wood.

Be Careful: Be very careful using the heated wood-burning tool. Don't leave the hot tool unattended, and make sure to shut it off between transfers.

7. Once you get the results you want on scrap wood, tape your wood block to a heat-resistant surface and your photocopy to one side of the block. Anchoring the wood and copy will help prevent the transfer from blurring. Use the wood-burning tool to transfer the photo onto the wood block. If you are not satisfied with the transfer, remove it with sandpaper and start again.

8. To give the "stone" some color, paint all sides of the block except the side with the transfer. Let the paint dry, and then use sandpaper to lightly distress the painted surfaces. Onto the painted surfaces only, brush antique medium and immediately wipe it off with a soft cloth. Seal all the surfaces with varnish or acrylic medium.

Tip: You may wish to test the paint color and the distressing and antiquing techniques on scrap wood before applying them to your wood block (see photo below).

9. About $1/8$"/3 mm in from either end of the ring band, mark the position of two holes (for inserting brads to set the "stone"). Using a #62 bit, drill a hole at each mark. Insert and position the wood block in the band. To prevent the wood from splitting when you add the brads, use a #71 bit inserted through the center of each hole in the band to predrill the wood to a depth of about $1/4$"/6 mm (or the depth to which each brad will penetrate the wood). Next, repeat this predrilling with a #62 bit, but this time barely drill into the wood (to only a partial depth to which each brad will penetrate the wood). Then, secure the wood "stone" in the ring by hammering a tiny copper brad into each hole.

Janette Schuster
(above)

Heart in Hand, 2003,
2¾ x 3½"/6.9 x 8.9 cm.
Tintype, cookie tin,
vintage metal ruler,
steel nails.

Tarnished Halo, 2003,
2¾ x 3½"/6.9 x 8.9 cm.
Tintype, cookie tin, rusted
bottle cap, watch parts,
glass beads.

"To create these two
pins, I pressed into
service the 'anonymous
ancestors' pictured in
the tintypes as stand-
ins for two of my
Scottish great-great
grandparents. Although
I know little about
them, I imagine them as
fallible humans, him
with his heart in his
hand and her with her
tarnished halo."

Stephanie Rubiano
(above)

Starstruck Pixie, 2003,
3¾ x 2"/9.5 x 5 cm.
Nickel silver, vintage tin,
decal, rivets.

"This piece was a gift of
friendship, custom made
for me by Stephanie in
remembrance of days
shared making art and
scouring antique stores
for vintage tins and
other collage materials."

Beth Piver
(above)

Starry Eyed Brooch, 2005, 4 x 1³/₄ x ¹/₂"/10.2 x 4.4 x 1.3 cm.
Nickel silver, copper, bronze, brass stampings, steel nuts and bolts, photo.

"This series of brooches in the form of what Beth calls her own 'bizarre little figures' was inspired by her fascination with the colorful characters of circuses and sideshows."

Beth Piver
(above)

Unicycle Brooch, 2003, 3¹/₂ x 2 x ¹/₂"/8.9 x 5 x 1.3 cm.
Nickel silver, copper, bronze, brass, found objects, steel nuts and bolts, photo, paint.

Ace Brooch, 2003, 4 x 2¹/₂ x ¹/₂"/10.2 x 6.4 x 1.3 cm.
Nickel silver, copper, bronze, brass, found objects, brass stampings, steel nuts and bolts, photo, paint.

Beth Piver
(above)

Little Devil Brooch, 2006, 3¹/₂ x 1¹/₄ x ¹/₂"/8.9 x 3.1 x 1.3 cm.
Nickel silver, copper, bronze, found objects, steel nuts and bolts, photo.

Roller Brooch, 2005, 4¹/₂ x 2¹/₄ x ³/₄"/11.4 x 2.6 x 1.9 cm.
Nickel silver, copper, bronze, brass, found objects, steel nuts and bolts, computer-generated photo.

Linda O'Brien
(above)

She Was a Traveling Girl, 2005, 2 1/8 x 1 3/8 x 1/8"/5.3 x 3.5 x .3 cm (with chain 15 1/4"/38.7 cm).
Copper, paper, plastic laminate, washers, found objects, eyelets.

"My Aunt Fran was the inspiration for this piece. She worked for the government, never married, and traveled most of her life, living in many fascinating countries. She was my mentor and greatest source of encouragement, and died at 91. She was a true original!"

Karen Strauss
(above)

Sea Dreams, 2007, 16"/40.6 cm (with chain).
Metal clay, antique postcard, mica, aquamarine beads, freshwater and cultured pearls, coral, shells, sterling silver findings.

"I live on a small Caribbean island by the sea. The colors of the ocean are my constant inspiration."

chapter four objects of affection

I AM A SELF-CONFESSED ITH (Incurable Treasure Hunter), and if you are reading this book, I'll bet you are one, too. Some might call us junkers, recyclers, scavengers, or just plain crazy, but I say we're collectors and users of found objects.

Many of the jewelry pieces you've seen so far in this book are made with *found objects*. A found object is a castoff of nature or man that can be repurposed in art or decoration for its aesthetic appeal. You might find one on a walk through the woods, in your basement, or in a thrift shop. It might be a natural object, such as a piece of driftwood or a feather, or a human-made item, such as a watch gear or spoon. If you can find it, acquire it, and use it in a new way, you have a found object.

Found objects can be vivid reminders of past events or emotions. Whether it's your grandfather's pocket watch, a shard of beach glass or shell from your vacation, the key to your first car, or your child's lost tooth, all of us collect souvenirs of our journey through life. We are memory magpies with at least a few found objects stashed away. These objects may be trash to some, but to us they are sentimental treasures worthy of repurposing in wearable art.

There are many, many kinds of found objects just waiting out there to be discovered and used in collage jewelry. Some of my favorites include ephemera (such as maps, tickets, journal pages, and book pages), typewriter and adding machine keys and other parts, food and storage tins, cutlery, watch and clock parts, keys, and rulers. Consider also shells, feathers, rocks, beads, broken pieces of jewelry, optical lenses and eye glasses, springs, bottle caps, metal stampings and scraps, charms, hinges, dice, and dog tags. The list of possibilities is just about endless. And so is the list of places you can locate

"Whether it's your grandfather's pocket watch, a shard of beach glass or shell from your vacation, the key to your first car, or your child's lost tooth, all of us collect souvenirs of our journey through life."

found objects. Keep your eyes open wherever you are, whether it is in a parking lot, at the hardware or dollar store, at a garage sale, at the recycling center or junkyard, on the beach, in a park, in your parent's attic, or in your own closet.

When searching for found objects, remember that you simply can't beat natural wear and patina for beauty. Watch for objects that show their age, but don't discount new items or those with a too-shiny finish. These objects can be distressed with sandpaper and aged with patina solution. Also, when collecting items for use in jewelry, keep the scale of the found objects in mind. Using objects that are too large can result in cumbersome jewelry, although how large constitutes "too large" is mostly a matter of personal taste. I wish you good hunting, fellow ITHs.

recycled treasures necklace

Artist: **Amy Hanna**

AMY HANNA HAS A unique talent for artfully assembling broken bits and pieces of Victorian jewelry into a wearable story. The title of this necklace, *Ina Loved to Gamble While Wearing Her Rubies*, reflects her vivid imagination and love of family. As Amy explains, "This piece was inspired by my great Aunt Ina's love of gambling while wearing her late husband's watch chain and her favorite ruby ring."

Materials

- Victorian "gem" tintype
- Vintage game piece or similar round object
- Vintage decorative brass button, earring, or similar round finding
- Two 24-gauge sterling silver head pins, at least 3"/7.6 cm long
- Two medium garnet or similar beads
- Four small beads or buttons, such as vintage rhinestone or crystal
- 22-gauge sterling silver wire, approximately 36"/91.4 cm
- Two pieces of large-link sterling silver chain, approximately 3"/7.6 cm each
- Two large garnet or similar beads
- Two pieces of medium-link sterling silver chain, approximately 3"/7.6 cm each
- Closure, such as large sterling silver hook and ring

- Brass or gold watch chain (antique or new), approximately 12"/30.5 cm
- Brass or gold watch chain (antique or new), approximately 10"/25.4 cm
- Two brass or gold watch swivels or other clasps, such as lobster clasps
- Celluloid circle or similar small plastic or metal ring (such as a curtain, Roman blind, or extra-large jump ring)
- Bar-shaped metal finding, such as a toggle clasp or bead spacer, approximately 2"/5 cm
- Antique silver medal or other charm
- Crystal or metal bead
- Small disk-shaped ruby or similar bead
- Small brass or gold jump rings (optional)

Tools and Supplies

- Adhesive of your choice
- Flush cutter
- Needle-nose pliers
- Patina kit with silver black patina solution
- Wire wrapping kit
- Drilling kit with ¹⁄₁₆"/1.5 mm drill bit (optional)

MAKE IT YOUR OWN

To make your own version, look for treasure to recycle at the bottom of your own jewelry box, and then ask your relatives if you can raid their jewelry boxes, too. Gather any jewelry pieces or parts that speak to you, whether they are antique, vintage, or new. Supplement your collection of recyclable jewelry by searching flea markets, antique stores, and thrift shops. Be sure to ask for broken jewelry, which often can be purchased at a discount. Use a tintype of your ancestor, as well as some found objects with personal meaning.

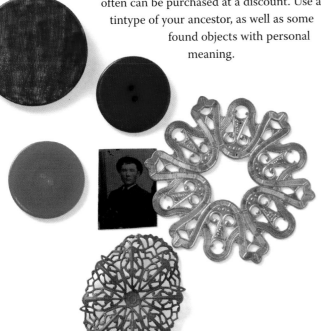

1. Choose a small Victorian tintype, called a *gem* tintype, to be the focal piece of the central pendant. (Or use a larger tintype and cut it down to size.) Look for a vintage game piece that can add color and support for the tintype. If you don't have a vintage game piece, try using a similar object, such as a poker chip, button, or craft wood circle you can paint any color you desire (see photo, left). Adhere the tintype to the game piece.
2. Look for a metal finding that is larger than the tintype and game piece and can be bent around these two pieces

to enclose them. Amy used a vintage button, but you can use any similar round object, such as a filigree stamping, brooch, or earring. Amy used a flush cutter to remove the shank from the button, and then used needle-nose pliers to bend parts of the button around the tintype and game piece (see photo page 93, bottom).

3. To darken and age any new or too shiny silver findings and wire, use a silver black patina solution, following the instructions on page 22.

Be Careful: Remember to work in a well-ventilated area when using patina solution.

4. Onto a silver head pin, thread a medium-sized bead, such as a vintage garnet bead, and four small rhinestone or similar beads or buttons (such as clear glass or crystal). Following the instruction on page 21, wire-wrap the head pin wire to the bottom of the tintype pendant. (If your pendant does not already have an opening through which to thread the wire, drill a small hole in the bottom of the pendant using a ¹⁄₁₆"/1.5 mm bit).

5. Use wire wrapping and 22-gauge sterling silver wire to attach a piece of large-link silver chain to the top of the tintype pendant. At the loose end of the chain, use wire wrapping to attach a length of silver wire. Onto this wire, thread a large garnet bead (see photo below), and then wire wrap the loose end of the wire to a piece of medium-link silver chain. Repeat this step to add a second piece of large-link silver chain, large garnet bead, and piece of medium-link silver chain to the top of the tintype pendant.

6. Use wire wrapping to attach each part of the closure to the loose ends of the medium-link chain. Amy used an extra-large hook and ring to add drama at the back of the piece.

7. To begin assembling the longer outer chain, attach a watch swivel to each watch chain (using a small jump ring or wire wrapping, if needed). Then use the swivels to clip the watch chains to the medium-link chains near the closure.

8. To the loose end of the 10"/25.4 cm watch chain, use a jump ring or wire wrapping to attach a found object circle or similar ring-shaped object (Amy used a vintage French celluloid circle). To the loose end of the 12"/30.5 cm watch chain, attach a bar-shaped metal finding (Amy used a vintage finding salvaged from a watch chain). Link the two watch chains by passing the bar-shaped finding through the circle, just like a toggle bar through a ring.

Tip: When choosing found objects for the circle and bar, remember that the bar must be able to pass through the circle and "catch" on the other side without easily passing back out. In other words, the circle and bar must function in the same way a toggle ring and bar closure does (see top photo, page 92). Also, you might need to drill one or two holes in the bar so you can attach it to the watch chain and, in step 9, to the crystal bead and medal.

9. Use wire wrapping to attach an antique medal to a crystal bead (see photo, right) and then to the center of the bar-shaped finding. Onto a silver head pin, thread a medium-size bead, such as a vintage garnet bead, and then a small disk-shaped bead. Use wire wrapping to attach the beads to the center of the bar-shaped finding.

Artist: **Stephanie Jones Rubiano**

STEPHANIE RUBIANO LOVES to make jewelry using both found objects and family photos. She explains, "This is one of my favorite photos of my grandmother as a young girl. The watch case frames her face perfectly, and the contemplative look she wears inspired the choice of the word *reverie*."

Materials

- Photo
- Vintage book page or other text
- Vintage wristwatch case
- Small crystal decorations, such as rhinestone stars or beads
- Two 24-gauge sterling head pins, approximately 1½"/3.8 cm
- Pearl beads
- Small sterling silver jump rings
- Sterling silver chain with clasp

Tools and Supplies

- Computer with imaging software, scanner, and printer
- Paper collage kit with PVA glue
- Resin kit
- Wire wrapping kit
- Drilling kit (optional)

MAKE IT YOUR OWN

To make your own version, use a photo of a family member or dear friend. If you don't already have a keepsake wristwatch case, purchase one at an online auction or antique store. From an old book page, cut out words that have meaning to you or that reflect the person in your photo.

1. Choose a photo. Scan it and, using your computer's imaging software, enhance it as desired and adjust its size to fit inside the watch case. Print out the photo. Cut it out around the outline of the person, if desired.

2. Select favorite words from a vintage book and cut out the text. Adhere the text to the printout with PVA glue and let it dry. Coat both sides of the collage with several thin coats of PVA glue, letting it dry completely between each coat. Use a small amount of glue to adhere the collage inside the watch case. Let the glue dry completely.

3. Follow the instructions for using resin on page 26. Pour the resin into the watch case and allow it to set overnight or until solid. Glue small crystal decorations to the surface of the resin as desired.

4. The wristwatch case should have two holes on either side, in which a watchband spring bar once sat. (If yours does not have holes, you will need to drill them.) Thread a head pin through the bottom hole on one side of the watch case, and then string enough pearl beads onto the head pin wire to fill up the space between the two holes. Thread the wire through the top hole (see photo above). Use the instructions for wire wrapping on page 21 to make a loop with a wrapped tail above the top hole.

Tip: If the holes in your pearl beads are too small for the head pin wire, use the instructions on page 71 to enlarge them.

5. Repeat step 4 for the second set of holes on the other side of the watch case. Use small jump rings to attach a chain to the pendant.

blue eyes charm bracelet

Artist: **Janette Schuster**

I MAY HAVE INHERITED my artistic abilities from my mom, but I got my love of tools from my dad. His workshop basement was a veritable hardware store of pliers, shears, sanders, and drills. He also had the most remarkable eyes of cornflower blue, which inspired this bracelet. In Dad's honor, I used found materials from the hardware store, as well as coins from his collection and a small locket containing his photo.

Materials

- Five to seven ¾"/1.9 cm zinc electrical conduit locknuts, loose or part of conduit connectors (plus one extra for practice drilling)
- Twelve to twenty-five large jump rings, approximately 5/16"/1.8 mm inner diameter (ID)
- Closure, such as pewter finish large lobster clasp with spring or jump ring
- Small jump ring, approximately 3/16"/5 mm ID (for attaching clasp)
- Found objects such as coins, gears, buttons, beads, and charms
- 24-gauge soft wire in light brown color or copper
- Seed beads

Tools and Supplies

- Drilling kit with drill press and 1/16"/1.5 mm cobalt bit
- Wire wrapping kit
- Bent-nose pliers
- Hammer
- Flush cutter
- Small file
- Digital camera (optional)
- Metal punch (optional)
- Patina kit with pewter black patina solution (optional)
- Clear nail polish, wax, or spray-on sealant (optional)

MAKE IT YOUR OWN

To make your own version, visit your local hardware store to see what objects you can find. Take your color inspiration from a parent's eyes or another personal source, and gather found objects of that color to use as charms.

1. I was drawn to the funky industrial look of electrical conduit locknuts, but the ridged variety I used might only be available attached to metal conduit connectors. If so, first remove the locknuts from the connectors by unscrewing them.

2. Using a drill press and 1/16"/1.5 mm cobalt bit, drill two holes on opposite sides of each locknut (for a total of four holes per locknut) as shown in the photo at right.

Tip: When you have many similar holes to drill, as in this case, a drill press is the tool to use. You can just set up the drill press to the position and speed that works best for you and drill hole after consistent hole in relatively short order. Do a drilling practice run first using an extra locknut or scrap metal.

3. To form a bracelet, link the drilled locknuts with jump rings. Attach a closure (as shown below). Try on the bracelet to test the length for fit before planning out your design. A slight adult's or child's wrist might require only four locknuts, whereas a larger adult's wrist will likely require six locknuts. Adjust the length of the

bracelet as needed by adding or removing locknuts or jump rings between the clasp and locknut.

Tip: Jump rings and drill bits can vary somewhat by brand in terms of gauge, or thickness. If you find that the links of your bracelet do not articulate smoothly, try using a slightly larger drill bit or thinner gauge jump ring.

4. Once you are satisfied with the length, lay the bracelet flat on a table and plan the arrangement of the found object charms. Gather round- or other-shaped objects that fit inside the locknuts with enough open space between the object and locknut to allow for attachment by wire wrapping. Consider found objects such as coins, wood hearts, and gears. If you wish, vary the kinds of metals used to include pewter, silver, copper, and brass. Stick to a limited color scheme, and discard any items that are not quite the right color. Once satisfied with your design, consider taking a digital photo to help you remember the arrangement of the objects. If needed, drill or punch holes in the objects for attaching them to the bracelet.

5. For ease in wire wrapping the objects to the locknuts, open the jump rings and take the links apart. If you wish, age the jump rings or found objects with pewter black patina solution (see page 22 for instructions). You might also want to coat the underside of the locknuts or any base metal findings with clear nail polish, wax, or a spray-on sealant to prevent skin irritation.

6. Cut the 24-gauge wire into lengths of about 5"/12.7 cm. Use wire wrapping (see page 21) to suspend the found objects inside the locknuts. For each object, first form wrapped loops through all the holes in the object. Wrap the wire around tightly only two or three times, to leave enough room for the second loop's wrapping (see photo above). Then, with the loose end of each wrapped wire, form a second loop to attach the object to a locknut. To keep the object in position without sliding around the locknut, aim for tightly closed loops and wrapped wires

rather than perfect looking loops (see photo below). If you find this challenging, keep practicing, and remember to use bent-nose pliers to tighten your wrapped coils and tuck in cut wire ends.

7. Use a combination of jump rings, head pins, and wire-wrapped loops to attach the found object charms. You might need to enlarge the existing holes in some manufactured charms using a 1/16"/1.5 mm bit in order to attach them with large jump rings. To make a head pin, splay one end of a piece of wire using a hammer. Cut the tip of the splayed end with a flush cutter, and file it just enough to smooth the rough edge. Thread on a seed bead to act as a "stopper," and then add a larger bead or button. Use wire wrapping to attach the head pin to a locknut, forming a loop large enough to allow the charm to move freely on the locknut.

8. Once all your found object charms are suspended from a locknut, reattach the links of the bracelet.

family silver pin and necklaces

Artist: **Janette Schuster**

LIKE A SOCK that has lost its mate, a single fork or spoon seems a bit forlorn separated from its matching set of family silverware. I like to rescue pieces of lost cutlery found at thrift stores and garage sales and give these silver-plated gems new lives as jewelry. Mix in a few family photos and you have this funny little family of three: a mom spoon necklace, a daughter spoon pin/pendant, and a dad fork necklace.

Materials

- Bezel cups or similar found containers
- Photos
- Embellishments such as skeletonized leaves, tiny gears, or mementos
- Sterling silver or silver-plated fork and two teaspoons
- Rivets such as #20 brass escutcheon pins or $\frac{1}{16}$"/1.5 mm copper rivets
- Brass and silver jump rings
- Two lobster clasps
- Two vintage or new brass watch chains
- Hanger for small pictures
- $1\frac{7}{8}$"/4.7 cm pin back with swivel
- Closure, such as lobster clasp and jump ring
- Small screw eye (optional)
- Adding machine key (optional)

Tools and Supplies

- Metal polish
- Soft cloth
- Computer with imaging software, scanner, and printer
- Paper collage kit with acrylic medium
- Resin kit
- Bench block
- Hammer
- Drilling kit with hand drill and #61, $\frac{1}{8}$"/3 mm, and $\frac{1}{16}$"/1.5 mm drill bits
- Ultrafine-point black permanent marker
- Sawing kit
- Finishing kit
- Awl
- Wire cutter
- Flat-nose pliers
- Metal shears
- Heat-resistant soldering surface
- Torch (such as propane)
- Bowl (for water bath)
- Round-nose pliers
- Colored pencils (optional)
- $\frac{1}{8}$"/3 mm metal punch (optional)

MAKE IT YOUR OWN

To make your own version, search your family archives (or a consignment shop) for photos and an odd piece or three of silverware handed down through the family. Consider using photos of your immediate family members, or use vintage postcard photos as I did. Instead of using the top of the spoon's handle as a charm, hang a memento of the family member pictured.

1. Gather and prepare bezel cups and other found containers to hold resin. I used manufactured brass bezel cups and the metal end caps of crescent roll containers. Remove any paper or cardboard stuck to the end caps. Also remove any rust or tarnish inside the cups or end caps, which may show through your photos. Clean the interior of each cup or end cap with a very small amount of metal polish following the manufacturer's instructions. Rinse and thoroughly remove any polish residue.

6. Drill or punch a $^1/_8$"/3 mm hole at the tip of the bowl (for attaching the chain). As shown below, mark the points where you will cut off the majority of the handle and the decorative tip of the handle (for the charm). Make the marked cuts using a jeweler's saw. Finish the cut edges until smooth. Using a $^1/_{16}$"/1.5 mm bit, drill coordinating holes in the remaining stub of the handle and the top of the charm for hanging.

7. On the surface of the resin filling the bezel cup, use an awl to mark the placement of two holes for rivets. Using a hand drill and #61 bit, carefully drill the holes through the resin-filled bezel cup (see photo page 103, top left). Position the bezel cup on the spoon and drill two coordinating holes. You can sign the back of the spoon at this time by stamping your name or initials in the metal. Carefully set two small rivets (such as #20 escutcheon pins) to attach the cup to the spoon.

2. Gather photos, and then enlarge or reduce them as needed using imaging software or a photocopier. Make a color photocopy of each photo, and enhance them using colored pencils if desired. Cut the photos to fit within the bezel cups or end caps.

3. To prevent the resin from lifting the image, thoroughly coat both sides and the edges of each photo with several thin coats of acrylic medium, letting the medium dry completely between coats. Use the medium to adhere each photo inside a bezel cup or end cap. Adhere any embellishments, such as skeletonized leaves, tiny gears, or mementos. (As you position the embellishments, keep in mind where you plan to place the rivets later.) Let the medium dry.

4. Following the instructions for using resin on page 26, mix and pour the resin into the bezel cups and end caps. Allow the resin to set overnight or until solid.

Mom Spoon Necklace

5. Place the bowl of a teaspoon on a bench block and hammer it until flat. Try hammering the back side first, and then flip back and forth between the front and back sides to hammer as needed. Bend or hammer the handle to straighten it. You may wish to clean the bowl or the entire spoon with polish, or leave it tarnished.

Tip: Resin can scratch or dent easily. While drilling or setting rivets in resin, work slowly and carefully. Minimize damage to the resin by covering it with paper or a soft cloth.

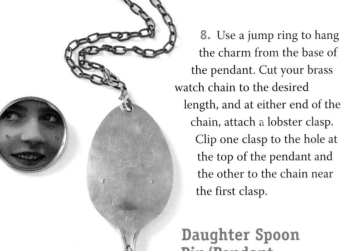

8. Use a jump ring to hang the charm from the base of the pendant. Cut your brass watch chain to the desired length, and at either end of the chain, attach a lobster clasp. Clip one clasp to the hole at the top of the pendant and the other to the chain near the first clasp.

Daughter Spoon Pin/Pendant

9. Repeat steps 5 and 6, but do not drill a hole at the tip of the spoon's bowl. To make the spoon both a pin and pendant, attach both a pin back and a fabricated bale. To make the bale, use flat-nose pliers to slightly bend a picture hanger (like those shown below, right) between its ring and stem. Use shears to cut off about half of the stem, and use a small file to finish the cut edge. Drill two holes in the stem. Position the hanger on the back of the spoon bowl near the top so it will not be visible from the front. Drill two coordinating holes in the spoon. Bevel the holes on the front of the spoon so the heads of the rivets will sit flush against the surface. Set the rivets to attach the hanger to the spoon. Repeat this step to attach the pin back, this time trimming the pin back and positioning it to sit in the middle of the spoon just below the bale, so it won't be visible from the front (see photo above).

10. Repeat steps 7 and 8, this time using a resin-filled end cap instead of a bezel cup, a $1/16$"/1.5 mm drill bit, and copper rivets. (If you wish, you can attach a similar chain to the pendant bale.)

Dad Fork Necklace

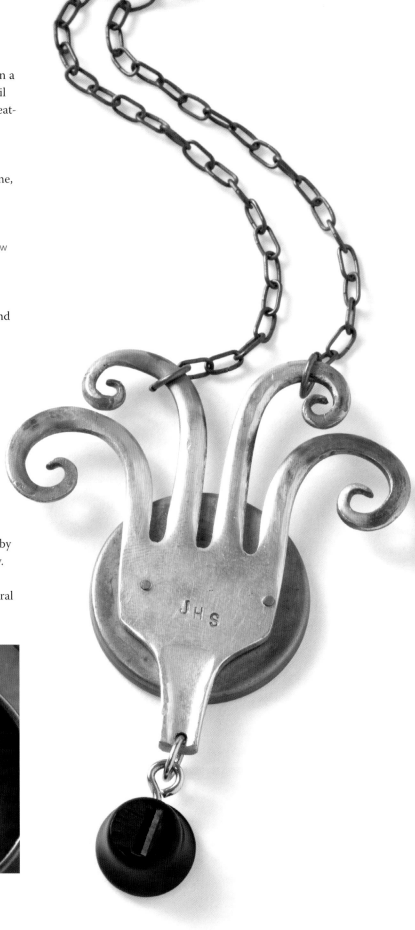

11. Place the head of a fork on a bench block and hammer it until flat. Then, place the fork on a heat-resistant surface. To anneal, or soften, the tines of the fork, use a torch to heat them until they glow a dull red. Remove them from the flame, and when the redness disappears, quench the fork in a water bath.

Be Careful: Remember to follow the safety precautions for using a torch on page 54.

12. Using sturdy round-nose pliers, bend the tines of the fork outward from the center (as shown, left) in any design you choose. Just be sure to close up curls of the two central tines to the point where jump rings can be placed on them without slipping off. Clean and finish the fork as desired using polish, files, and steel wool.

13. Mark, saw, and drill the handle of the fork as described in step 6. Next, repeat step 7 to attach a resin-filled bezel cup to the fork.

14. Use a jump ring to hang a charm from the base of the pendant. Use part of the cut fork handle as a charm, or use a memento, such as the charm I made by attaching a small screw eye to an adding machine key. Cut two pieces of brass watch chain to the desired length, and use jump rings to attach them to the central tines of the fork. Add a closure to the chain.

baby spoon necklace

Artist: **Janette Schuster**

PIECES OF MINIATURE SILVERWARE, such as doll and baby spoons, are often just the right size for use in jewelry. I made this necklace as a birthday gift for a new grandparent using photos from their childhood and a diminutive spoon.

Materials

- Small sterling silver or silver-plated spoon, such as a teaspoon or baby spoon
- Thin glass (such as slide binder glass or microscope slides), approximately 2"/5 cm square
- Two photos of children
- Collage papers, such as dictionary or other text pages
- 22-gauge copper sheet, approximately 1½ x 2"/3.8 x 5 cm
- Rivets such as #20 steel wire brads
- #1, #2, or #3 ball (or bead) chain, 2"/5 cm in aged copper
- 24-gauge copper wire
- Pearl seed beads
- Pearl bead
- Copper jump ring
- Copper chain with closure

Tools and Supplies

- Bench block
- Hammer
- Metal polish
- Soft cloth
- Drilling kit with #61 and ¹⁄₁₆"/1.5 mm drill bits
- Ultrafine-point black permanent marker
- Sawing kit
- Finishing kit
- Glass cutting kit
- Paper collage kit
- Photocopier or computer with imaging software, scanner, and printer
- Soldering kit
- Paper
- Rubber cement
- Ruler
- Metal stamps

- Patina kit with gun blue or pewter black patina solution
- Safety glasses
- Rubber gloves
- Double-sided foam tape
- Ceramic tile, recycled or new
- Wire wrapping kit
- ¹⁄₁₆"/1.5 mm metal punch (optional)
- Sanding block (optional)

MAKE IT YOUR OWN

To make your own version, use photos of the newest member in your family to celebrate the birth of a child. Or, use childhood photos of a favorite uncle or grandparent. If you don't have a baby spoon, use a tiny teaspoon as I did. You can also find similar small silverware at an antique mall.

1. Place the bowl of a small spoon on a bench block and hammer it until flat. Try hammering the back side first, and then flip back and forth between the front and back sides to hammer as needed. Bend or hammer the handle to straighten it. You might want to clean the bowl or the entire spoon with polish, or leave it tarnished.

2. Drill or punch a ¹⁄₁₆"/1.5 mm hole at the tip of the handle for hanging the pendant. Use a marker to sketch two half circles or ovals at opposite ends of the spoon's bowl. Drill a hole inside each half circle, and then use a jeweler's saw to cut out the rest (see leftmost spoon in photo at right). Finish the cut edges using small files and steel wool.

3. Cut two pieces of glass (see page 27 for instructions) to the same size, about ³⁄₄ x ³⁄₄"/1.9 × 1.9 cm or any other size that fits on the spoon's bowl. You might want to use

sketch and use rubber cement to adhere it to the copper sheet. Let the adhesive dry, and then use a jeweler's saw to cut out the arch. Finish the cut edges, and use fine steel wool to clean the top surface.

7. Measure and mark the center of the arch. Stamp, or chase, the phrase "child's play" or any word, phrase, or name with meaning to you, using the center mark to help you position the letters on the arch.

8. Treat the copper with a patina solution until the letters blacken (following the instructions on page 22). To make the letters stand out, gingerly clean the surface around the letters with steel wool or a kitchen scouring pad.

9. Cut a piece of double-sided foam tape the same size as the window you will cut in the spoon's bowl. Adhere the tape over the part of the charm you want revealed through the window, then position and tape the charm on the front of the spoon. Use an ultrafine-point marker

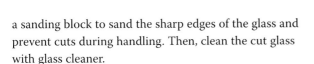

a sanding block to sand the sharp edges of the glass and prevent cuts during handling. Then, clean the cut glass with glass cleaner.

4. Prepare two small collages. Choose two photos, one for either side of the soldered charm. Use imaging software or a photocopier to reduce the photos to fit within the dimensions of the cut glass. Print out each image, and then use small, sharp scissors to cut out the outlines of the people (see photo above).

5. Choose a background paper, such as a dictionary page. Follow steps 5–9 on page 46 (Soldered Charm Earrings) to create a two-sided collage sandwiched between the two pieces of glass. Then, to form a soldered charm, tape and solder the glass "sandwich" following the instructions on page 29.

6. On a piece of paper, sketch an arch-shaped embellishment similar to the one pictured in photo (top right) that is sized for your spoon. Roughly cut out the

11. Cut two pieces of ball chain to a length equal to the width of the charm (see photo page 107, bottom). Clean the ball chain with steel wool, and then flux it and the top and bottom edges of the charm. Working on a ceramic tile, use foam tape to help anchor the charm snugly against the chain (as described on pages 46–47). Use a soldering iron to solder the chain to the charm. Be sure to remove any remaining flux.

12. Use nail polish remover to clean any marker remaining on the spoon. Position and clamp the charm on the spoon, and lightly flux it and the spoon below it in a few spots. At these spots, solder the charm to the spoon. Remove any remaining flux and finish the surface as desired.

13. Follow the instructions on page 99 to make a head pin from copper wire. Thread a pearl seed bead, a pearl bead, and another pearl seed bead on the head pin. Use wire wrapping to attach it to the base of the pendant. Finally, use a jump ring to attach a chain with a closure to the pendant.

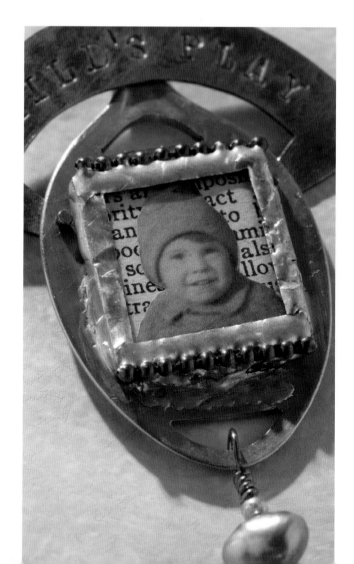

to trace around the outside of the charm. Carefully remove the charm, leaving the tape adhered to the spoon. Trace around the tape and then remove it. Use a saw to cut out the window along the tape tracing line. Finish the cut edges.

10. Use the charm tracing line to plan the position of the arch and the two rivets that will attach it to the spoon. Mark the position of two rivet holes outside the line. Trim the ends of the arch if needed so it will not overlap the charm. Using a #61 bit, drill two holes in the spoon and the coordinating holes in the arch. Set the rivets.

pocket watch case necklace

Artist: **Janette Schuster**

EVEN TINY VACATION KEEPSAKES, no matter how humble, deserve to be kept in a place of honor. Pocket watch cases with their glass-enclosed chambers make ideal souvenir keepers. I collaged my own beachcombing vacation finds, a vintage photo, and beads from my mom's earring inside an antique pocket watch case and suspended it from a necklace of vintage and new beads.

Materials

- Vintage or new pocket watch case
- Photo or other background paper
- Small mementos such as shells, star fish, and beads
- Translucent beading cord, approximately 26"/66 cm
- Two double cup (or clam shell) bead tips
- Assorted glass seed and larger beads in colors of your choice
- Large central bead, approximately ½"/1.3 cm
- Closure, such as screw clasp
- Two pieces small-link chain, approximately ¹³⁄₁₆"/2.1 cm each
- Two medium jump rings (to fit over seed beads)
- Two small jump rings
- Head pin

Tools and Supplies

- Metal polish
- Soft cloth
- Paper
- Pencil
- Paper collage kit with heavy gel medium
- Super glue
- Clear nail polish
- Wire wrapping kit
- Needle or tweezers
- Patina kit (optional)
- Beading board (optional)

MAKE IT YOUR OWN

To make your own version, use a family heirloom or purchased pocket watch case. Gather your own mementos that are small enough to fit inside the case (consider shells, baby teeth, a lock of hair, pebbles, photos, or lace). Reuse beads from your broken jewelry, or purchase new ones.

1. Remove the glass cover from the pocket watch case. Clean and polish the watch case inside and out, if desired. If you are using a new case, consider aging the piece by treating it with a patina solution (as described on page 22).

2. Make a template for your collage. Trace around the outside of the case (or the cover), and cut out the tracing. Test the fit by inserting the template in the case, and trim it as needed.

3. Choose a photo or other paper for the background of your collage. You might use decorative paper or text. Use the template to cut the photo to size (see photo below). Test the fit, trim as needed, and then glue the photo inside of the case using gel medium.

4. Gather small mementos that fit inside the case. I used a shell, a star fish, and vintage beads. Arrange the mementos as desired and use heavy gel medium to adhere them inside the case. Let the gel medium dry. Reattach the cover of the watch case.

5. Decide what length your necklace will be (mine is about 16"/40 cm). Cut the beading cord to that length plus an extra 10"/25 cm (to allow for knots and mistakes).

6. At one end of the cord, tie a knot larger than the hole in the bead tip (so it won't slip through). I suggest using a figure eight knot. To tie this knot, first form a loop and then another loop to create an 8. Thread the end of the cord through the first loop, and pull the knot tight. Secure the knot with a drop of super glue and let the glue dry.

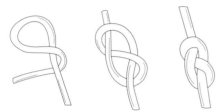

7. Make a fresh, sharp cut at the opposite end of the cord. To form a built-in beading needle, dip this end in nail polish, scrape off any excess polish, and let it dry.

8. Thread a bead tip on the cord so the knot is snug inside the cups. Trim the excess cord beyond the knot, and then close the cups around the knot with your fingers or pliers.

9. Plan the arrangement of beads for your necklace, using a beading board if desired. I used a combination of vintage and new glass seed and larger beads. Vary the bead sizes and shapes, separating larger beads with seed beads. Make the necklace symmetrical, with one large bead at the center surrounded on either side by two seed beads. Once you are satisfied with your design, string the beads on the cord.

Tip: At garage sales and flea markets, I snap up damaged vintage earrings, necklaces, and bracelets containing faceted crystal beads, then reuse the beads in jewelry. You can also purchase similar reproduction beads through bead and jewelry suppliers.

10. Thread a second bead tip on the cord with the cups opening outward away from the beads. Tie a figure eight knot, this time using a needle or tweezers to tighten and snug the knot against the bead tip. Trim the excess cord beyond the knot, and secure it with a drop of super glue. Close the cups around the knot. Attach a closure to the necklace.

Tip: Be consistent with the type or color of metal findings you use throughout the piece. If your watch case is gold, use all gold or gold-colored findings. If your case is silver, use all sterling or silver-colored findings.

11. Cut two pieces of chain of equal length. Use two medium jump rings to suspend the pieces on either side of the central bead, and use two small jump rings to attach the watch case to the chains. Adjust the length of the chains as needed, removing one link at a time.

12. Your watch case might have a loop at the bottom from which you can suspend a charm. To make a beaded charm, thread a small bead on a head pin. Trim the head pin wire and use pliers to form a loop. Attach the wire loop to the loop at the bottom of the watch case.

casino bracelet

Artist: **Phoenix Forrester**

OUR ENVIRONMENTS PROVIDE us not only with found objects but also with the inspiration for using them. The casinos springing up around Phoenix Forrester in her home state of New Mexico inspired this colorful charm bracelet, entitled *Lucky Me*.

Materials

- Vintage or new playing cards with a shiny coated (not matte) finish
- Vintage or new dice in assorted sizes and colors
- Six to ten sterling silver bezel cups in assorted shapes and sizes, approximately ½ to 1"/1.3 to 2.5 cm
- Twelve to twenty small sterling silver jump rings
- Micro glitter
- Sterling silver charm bracelet with closure
- Three to five sterling silver head pins, approximately 1¾"/4.4 cm

Tools and Supplies

- Advanced soldering kit with easy silver solder
- Pencil
- Paper scissors
- Industrial adhesive
- Resin kit
- Drilling kit
- Wire wrapping kit

MAKE IT YOUR OWN

To make your own version, scavenge playing cards, dice, and other game pieces from your own or your children's game collection. Games that are missing a few pieces and incomplete decks of cards can be purchased at bargain prices from thrift stores and secondhand shops. Consider including other found trinkets with personal meaning.

1. Gather playing cards and dice. Look for colorful cards, particularly face cards and those with pictures. Phoenix looks for old celluloid, Bakelite, and bone dice at flea markets and antique shops. Plan your design around a color, suit of cards, or other theme.

2. Purchase bezel cups in an assortment of sizes and shapes, if you desire. Consider using round, square, rectangular, oval, heart-shaped, and triangular bezel cups. Flux each bezel cup and a coordinating jump ring, and then use a torch and easy solder to attach the jump rings to the bezel cups (see photo below).

3. Clean and polish the bezels cups using the method of your choice (see page 23).

4. Lay each bezel cup over the part of a playing card you want to include in a charm, and trace the bezel cups with a pencil. Cut out each tracing and use a small amount of industrial adhesive to glue it inside its matching bezel cup (see photo below). Let the glue dry.

5. Follow the instructions for using resin on page 26. Carefully fill each bezel cup with resin and sprinkle a tiny amount of micro glitter into the wet resin as desired. Allow the resin to set overnight or until solid.

6. Using a drill bit of an appropriate size for your head pins, drill a hole through each of the dice.

7. Lay an open charm bracelet on your work surface. Arrange the resin charms and dice beside the bracelet (see photo, right). Attach each resin charm to the bracelet with a jump ring. Thread each die on a head pin and use wire wrapping (see page 21) to attach all the dice to the bracelet.

naturalist badge

Artist: **Bryan Petersen**

BRYAN PETERSEN'S PASSION for recycling and the environment is reflected in his jewelry. He says, "I try to use most of the items in my recycling bin, and this badge is probably 80 percent recycled material. My goal is to create wearable, attractive, and sustainable jewelry."

Materials

- Bottle cap
- Two decorative food tins (such as olive oil, tomato, or cookie tins)
- ¾"/1.9 cm pin back with two holes
- 26-gauge steel wire, approximately 4"/10.2 cm
- Jump ring
- 18-gauge brass wire, approximately 1"/2.5 cm

Tools and Supplies

- Ruler
- Pencil
- Scrap wood block, approximately 3½ x 3½/8.9 x 8.9 cm and at least ½"/1.3 cm thick
- Drawing compass
- Medium ball peen hammer
- Metal shears or tin snips
- Can opener
- Finishing kit

- Paper
- Paper scissors
- Rubber cement
- Drilling kit with #56 and #45 drill bits
- Sawing kit
- Chain-nose pliers
- Ultrafine-point permanent marker
- Flat-nose pliers
- Wire cutter
- Bone folder or other burnishing tool
- Small ball peen hammer

MAKE IT YOUR OWN

To make your own version, check for buried treasure in your own recycling bin. Why not use a bottle cap from a favorite beverage or a food tin in your favorite color?

1. Use a ruler to draw lines from corner to corner across the top of the scrap wood block. Where the lines intersect is the center of the block. With a compass, draw a 1⅛"/2.8 cm diameter circle at the center of the block. Place it on a firm surface or concrete floor, and use a medium ball peen hammer to sink the wood slightly within the circled area (see photo below).

2. Place a bottle cap on the circle with the interior of the cap (the unprinted side) facing up. Holding the cap by the crinkled rim, use a medium ball peen hammer to hit and shape the cap into a dome. Hammer around the inside of the cap, rotating and angling the cap as needed within the circular depression of the block. Strike where the flat center of the cap meets the crinkled rim, stretching the crinkles to create a uniform dome. Remove any plastic coating remaining inside of the bottle cap.

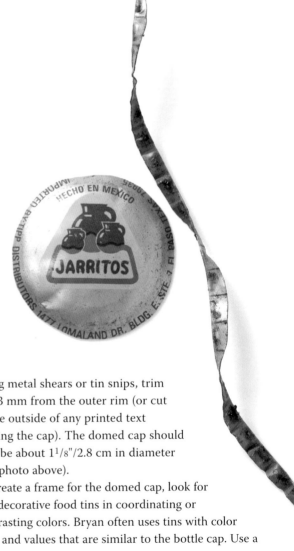

3. Using metal shears or tin snips, trim ⅛"/3 mm from the outer rim (or cut to the outside of any printed text circling the cap). The domed cap should now be about 1⅛"/2.8 cm in diameter (see photo above).

4. To create a frame for the domed cap, look for two decorative food tins in coordinating or contrasting colors. Bryan often uses tins with color hues and values that are similar to the bottle cap. Use a

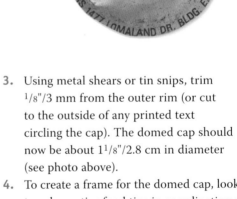

can opener and metal shears to cut the tins into sheets. Use the compass to make a donut-shaped template on paper by drawing a $1^1/4$"/3.1 cm circle with a $^{13}/_{16}$"/2.1 cm circle in the center. Roughly cut out the template, and use rubber cement to adhere it to one of the tin sheets. Let the rubber cement dry. Cut the outside circle with metal shears or tin snips. Drill a hole in the center, and use a jeweler's saw to cut out the $^{13}/_{16}$"/2.1 cm center circle (see photo above, middle). Finish the edges of the frame with a file until smooth.

5. Place the frame with its unprinted side facing up in the depression of the block. Hammer and shape the frame into a dome (as shown above, right), carefully holding it along the edge and rotating it until it fits over the bottle cap.

6. To create a backing piece for the badge, use sheet metal cut from the second tin in step 4. Make a photocopy of the template (bottom, right), roughly cut it out, and use rubber cement to adhere it to the unprinted side of the tin. Let the rubber cement dry. Use metal shears or tin snips to cut the tin along the outside circle of the template. Finish the cut edge.

7. Use chain-nose pliers to crimp and shape the tin circle until it resembles a small pie pan. Place the tip of the pliers at the middle or intermediate (not the innermost) circle line of the template. As you close the pliers to crimp the outside edge of the tin, bend the edge slightly toward the printed side of the tin. Work your way around the outside edge, crimping and bending about every $^1/_8$"/3 mm. When the crimped edge is complete, you should have a backing piece shaped like a shallow pie pan (see photo at right, top).

8. Now use the shears or snips to cut pairs of slits that cross like an X from the outer edge inward up to the innermost circle line. Using the template as a guide, continue cutting slits around the edge until you have eight equally spaced Xs (see photo below, middle). When you cross the cuts, you remove a small triangle-shaped piece and leave a triangle-shaped prong (which will be pushed up from the back to create a prong setting for the bottle cap and frame in step 11).

9. Use the two adjacent dots on the template as a guide to position a $^3/_4$"/1.9 cm pin back on the unprinted side of the backing piece. The pin back should be centered within the top third of the backing piece, so that one of the crimped petals is directly below the pin back at six o'clock. Mark onto the template the position of the two holes in the pin back. Using a #56 drill bit, drill the two holes. Remove the template.

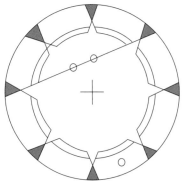

10. Cut two 2"/5 cm pieces of 26-gauge steel wire. Put the two wires together, form them into a "U" shape, and thread the tips through the holes in the pin stem and then through the holes in the backing piece. Use flat-nose pliers to pull and twist the wires until the pin back and backing piece are tightly attached. Trim the excess wire to $1/4$"/6 mm and bend the ends flush with the face of the backing piece (see photo below).

11. Working from the printed front of the backing piece, use flat-nose pliers to grab the prongs and bend them 90 degrees from the surface, creating a pronged setting. Drop the bottle cap into the setting, and then position the frame over the bottle cap. Using a bone folder or burnishing tool, set one prong and then the prong on the opposite side. Continue in this manner until all the prongs are set.

12. At the edge of the petal at six o'clock, mark and drill a hole using a #45 drill bit. Attach a jump ring at the hole.

13. Create a wire hanger from a 1"/2.5 cm piece of 18-gauge brass wire. At either end of the wire, use the flat-nose pliers to grasp and bend $1/4$"/6 mm of the wire at a 90-degree angle. Then, use chain-nose pliers to form a loop on either end.

14. Onto the unprinted side of a colorful tin sheet, use a marker to sketch a simple leaf outline similar to the one in the photo at right, top. The leaf should be symmetrical and measure about $1 3/8 \times 1/2$"/3.5 × 1.3 cm with a $1/8 \times 1/8$"/3 × 3 mm stem. Use shears or snips to cut out the leaf. Use flat-nose pliers to fold the leaf

along the center toward the printed side, creating about a 90-degree angle. Burnish the fold to make it crisp.

15. Set one half of the leaf printed-side down on the edge of the scrap wood block. Use a small ball peen hammer to indent and shape that half of the leaf as shown in the right hand photo at the bottom. Turn the leaf and shape the other half. Next, set the entire leaf printed-side down on the block and tap lightly along the folded spine to open the leaf a bit.

16. Set the looped wire in the crease of the leaf's stem. Use the flat-nose pliers to roll one side of the stem flange over the wire, and then roll the remaining flange over that. Use the jump ring to hang the leaf's outside loop from the badge.

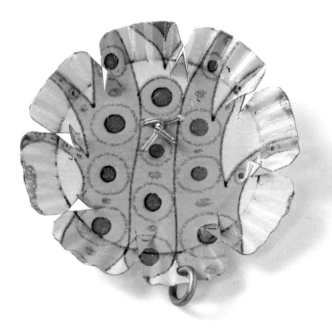

Stephanie Rubiano
(above)

Serene Dignity, 2007,
3³/₄ x 1¹/₄ x 1"/9.5 x 3.1 x 2.5 cm.
Silver-plated spoon, tintype, watch parts, brass eyelets and screws, sterling silver wire, paper, vintage tin.

"I purchased this unique spoon while antiquing with a friend, knowing it would provide a lovely backdrop for a small tintype. When I wear this piece, it reminds me of that wonderful visit and time well spent with a good friend."

Stephanie Rubiano
(above)

Enter Prospero, 2007,
2¹/₄ x 1⁵/₈ x ¹/₄"/5.6 x 4.1 x .6 cm.
Pocket watch face, optician's lens, milagro, steel rivets, paper.

"The base of this piece came from a pocket watch that belonged to my grandfather. He used to let me sit in his lap and help him wind it, so whenever I look at this piece, those cherished memories are relived."

Keith Lo Bue
(above)

Two Hundred Mistakes, 2001, 4³/₄ x 3 x 6"/12.1 x 7.6 x 15.2 cm.

Daguerreotype case, steel wire, optometrist's test lens, steel-point engraving, brass lion's head, 16th-century paper, eucalyptus nut, key, paper, text, leather, bead, soil.

"Each piece I work on will test or refine a particular technique, as a sideline to the greater importance of creating something that 'works' aesthetically and narratively."

Opie O'Brien
(above)

Maestro, 2006, 1 x ¹/₂ x ¹/₈"/2.5 x 1.3 x .3 cm.

Flute key, vintage tin can fragment, resin, cord.

"As a musician, this discarded old flute key really spoke to me and was the inspiration for this piece."

Alison Woodward
(above)

North and South, 2006,
32 x ¼"/81.3 x .6 cm.
Brass and enamel
pendants, glass beads,
reassembled brass links,
gold chain.

"My inspiration comes
from the thrill of
finding my materials
and the challenge of
assembling something
entirely new in such a
way as to highlight
the most interesting
features."

Alison Woodward
(above)

Pirate's Treasure, 2007,
31 x ½"/78.7 x 1.3 cm.
White wood, blue glass,
brass beads and chain,
white painted chain, brass
and rhinestone flower,
enamel pendant.

Alison Woodward
(above)

Coo-Coo, 2006,
29 x ½"/73.7 x 1.3 cm.
Brass chain, painted
metal, paper and glass
clock, aluminum fringe.

chapter five

I LOVE TO VISIT art museums, art galleries, and artist Web sites, because one of the things that inspires and teaches me the most is the work of talented artists. From the paintings of the old masters to the jewelry of modern innovators, works of art manifest the skill and imagination of their makers. Seeing the fruit of such skill and creativity educates me and inspires me to gather my own art tools and materials and see where they will take me.

As sources of education and inspiration, the projects in this chapter don't disappoint. They are a bit more challenging than those of preceding chapters. They are for intermediate to advanced jewelry artists, or those with hands-on experience using a jeweler's saw and soldering metal with a torch. However, beginning and experienced jewelry artists alike can find inspiration in the materials used by three master jewelry artists and their skillful methods of combining them.

In this final chapter, Marlene True, Thomas Mann, and Kristin Diener take collage materials that speak to them, apply their design experience and masterful jewelry-making skills, and create memory masterpieces. Marlene True, a skilled jewelry artist working toward a graduate degree under Robert Ebendorf, elevates the humble tin can to wearable high art. Artist and entrepreneur Thomas Mann, whose designs and execution of those designs are unsurpassed, works magic while mixing metals, images, and small keepsakes. Lastly, jewelry master Kristin Diener assembles travel mementos as eclectic as eyeglass lenses, road maps, and candy wrappers into treasure-encrusted adornments. I hope you find their creations as inspirational and educational as I do.

> "Seeing the fruit of such skill and creativity educates me and inspires me to gather my own art tools and materials and see where they will take me."

conversation ring | Artist: **Marlene True**

ART SPEAKS TO US, and sometimes it even starts a conversation. Marlene True's rings have something personal to say. Attracted to the color, narrative, and iconic images of tin cans, Marlene uses text cut from tin cans given to her by family and friends and incorporates them into her jewelry. She says of her work, "I like playing with the text from tin cans, as the words take on new meaning when removed from their original context."

Materials

- 22-gauge sterling silver ring blank, flat inside
- Tin cans with text printed on them
- 18-gauge (or 1 mm) sterling silver square wire
- 20-gauge sterling silver round wire

Tools and Supplies

- Ring gauge
- Paper
- Paper scissors
- Pencil
- Utility knife
- Heavy cardstock
- Can opener
- Metal shears
- Ring mandrel
- Rawhide mallet
- Caliper
- Ultrafine-point black permanent marker
- Sawing kit
- Advanced soldering kit

- Safety glasses
- Pickle supplies (see page 131)
- Finishing kit
- Bench block
- Nonserrated metal scissors or shears
- Masking tape
- Metal punch
- Ring clamp
- Drilling kit with a #68 or #69 drill bit, $^5/_{64}$"/2 mm ball bur, and #4 high-speed cylinder bur
- Small cross peen hammer
- Chasing hammer
- Silver polishing cloth

MAKE IT YOUR OWN

To make your own version, collect tins printed with text, such as olive oil, coffee, candy, and vegetable tins. Choose text that has significance to you, such as the name of a family member or a favorite food, city, state, or slogan.

1. Use a ring gauge to determine your ring size. Purchase a sterling silver ring blank in your size (or make a ring band using 22-gauge sterling silver sheet). Cut a band of paper the same width as your ring band. Wrap the band around the ring, mark where the paper meets, and then cut at the mark. Using a utility knife, cut a rectangular template window in heavy cardstock the size of the paper band.

2. Select a tin with text that you would like to use. Use a can opener and metal shears to cut a sheet of metal from the tin. Lay the template window over the tin to make sure that the text you have selected will work for the ring. Set aside your chosen tin text.

3. The silver ring band will become the liner band of your finished ring. Place it on the ring mandrel, and lightly tap it with a mallet to make it perfectly round. While the band is still on the mandrel, measure the diameter of the band with a caliper. Remove the band from the mandrel. Keep the caliper open to the diameter of the ring, and slide the caliper onto the ring mandrel until it fits and stops sliding. Read the ring size marked on the mandrel at the point that the caliper stops.

This measurement is the ring size for the two square wire rings you will create in step 4. Use the following chart to determine the length to cut the square wire:

Ring Size Indicated on Mandrel	Length in mm to Cut Square Wire
5	55.24
5$^1/_2$	56.54
6	57.74
6$^1/_2$	59.04
7	60.24
7$^1/_2$	61.54
8	62.84
8$^1/_2$	64.04
9	65.34
9$^1/_2$	66.54
10	67.84

4. Make two narrow metal bands to use as side rails for your band of tin text. Use the caliper to mark two pieces of 18-gauge (or 1 mm) sterling silver square wire to the length you read in the chart above. Use a jeweler's saw to

cut the two wire pieces, and use the mallet to form each wire around the ring mandrel. Flux the edges of each wire, and then use a torch and hard solder to solder the edges together to form a band (as shown, right). Once the two bands are soldered, place them in pickle until clean (to learn about pickle, see page 133), and then file away any excess solder from the inside of each ring. Place one band on the mandrel and tap lightly with a rawhide mallet to make it perfectly round. Repeat for the second wire band. Make sure your side rails are perfectly flat by placing them on a bench block and tapping them flat with the mallet.

Be Careful: When soldering, work in a well-ventilated area and use care when working with the flame. Pull back and secure long hair. Wear safety glasses and keep a fire extinguisher nearby.

5. Insert the liner band into one of the side rail bands. This should be a very tight fit. You may have to use a rawhide mallet to lightly hammer the liner band down into the side rail. If the side rail is too small, place it on the mandrel and gently hammer it with the rawhide mallet to make it slightly larger but not so large that it fits loosely over the liner.

6. Flux the outside edge of the band and the inside edge where the channel will be. With the outside edge facing up, lay medium solder on the outside edge and solder the bands together. Place the soldered bands in pickle until clean.

7. Repeat steps 5 and 6 to attach the second side rail on the other side of the liner band, but this time use easy solder. Next, finish and polish the ring inside and out using the method of your choice (see page 23).

8. Using a caliper, measure the width of the channel between the two side rails to determine the appropriate width of the band of tin. Using a mallet and bench block, hammer the tin flat. Use the utility knife to scribe the strip of tin to be cut. The band should be the same width as the channel, and the same length plus at least $1/8$"/3 mm as the liner band and paper band in step 1 (as shown below). Cut the tin with nonserrated metal scissors or shears.

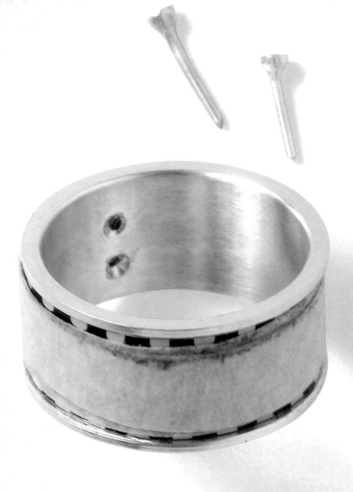

12. Cut a piece of 20-gauge round wire about 2"/5 cm long. Use a torch to heat one end of the wire until it begins to form a ball. Flip the wire over and form a ball on the other end. Pickle and polish the wire, then file the tops of the balls flat. Use a saw to cut the wire in the middle to form two rivets. Feed one rivet through one of the drilled holes from the inside toward the outside of the ring. Make sure the ball rests in the interior beveled hole, even if a large portion of the ball sticks out from hole. Carefully slide the ring over the ring mandrel so that it tightly holds the rivet in place. (If necessary, remove and cut down the rivet to leave only about $1/32$"/.8 mm of wire sticking above the tin.) Using first a small cross peen hammer and then the ball side of a chasing hammer, set the rivet. Repeat this step for the second rivet.

13. Using a #4 high-speed cylinder bur, carefully grind away the excess at the ball end of the rivet on the inside of the ring. Again, on the inside of the ring, sand the rivet heads until they are flush with the inside of the band.

14. Slide the ring on a mandrel. Using the small cross peen hammer, create texture by hammering the side rails of the channel. Polish the ring with a silver polishing cloth. Remove the tape.

9. File the corners of the cut tin to round them slightly. Using your fingers, form and bend the tin strip around a ring mandrel to the appropriate size. Remove the tin from the mandrel, wrap it around the ring inside the channel, and check the fit. File the tin to adjust the fit if necessary. Make sure the ends of the tin strip overlap at least $1/8$"/3 mm.

10. Cut a piece of masking tape the width and length plus about $3/4$"/1.9 cm of your tin strip. Use the tape to tightly secure the tin in the channel and protect it from scratching as you rivet and finish the ring.

11. With the tin in place in the channel, place the ring on a ring mandrel. Where the ends of the tin strip overlap and about $1/16$"/1.5 mm in from the exposed end, use a sharp center punch to make two dimples where the rivets will go. Place the ring in a ring clamp, and use a #68 or 69 drill bit to drill two holes through the tape, tin, and silver. Remove the ring from the clamp and use a $5/64$"/2 mm ball bur to create two countersinks on the inside of the ring in which the rivet heads will sit (shown above).

found object sandwich pin

Artist: **Thomas Mann**

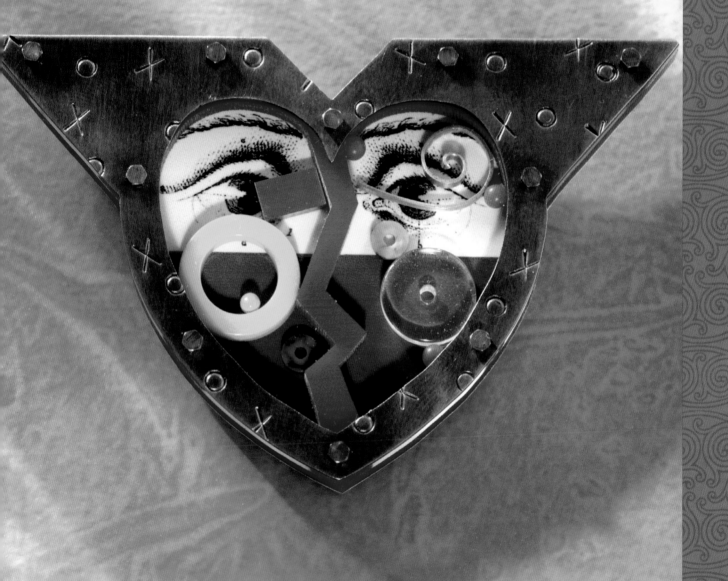

JEWELRY INNOVATOR THOMAS MANN is perhaps best known for his Techno Romantic designs, which combine industrial materials and romantic themes. He layered found and new materials into what he calls a "found object sandwich" to create this multipurpose piece that is a pin, pendant, and box for holding mementos.

Materials

- 22-gauge nickel silver sheet
- ¹⁄₁₆"/1.5 mm clear acrylic sheet
- ⅛"/3 mm red acrylic sheet
- Image or photo
- 26-gauge patterned brass sheet
- 16-gauge copper rivets
- Pin back with stem
- Small mementos or found objects
- 0-80 x ½"/1.3 cm hex head bolts and nuts
- Two necklace tabs (optional)
- Two 0-80 washers (optional)
- Necklace chain (optional)

Tools and Supplies

- Photocopier
- Paper scissors
- Rubber cement
- Sawing kit
- Drilling kit with #52 and #55 drill bits
- Bench block
- Stamps or chasing tools
- Chasing or other hammer
- Small-nose pliers
- Finishing kit
- Riveting kit
- 0-80 tap
- Miniature nut driver (optional)
- Flush cutter (optional)
- Patina kit with silver blackener (optional)

MAKE IT YOUR OWN

To make your own version, use an image or photo with personal meaning, and stash those small keepsakes you've been saving inside the heart-shaped box.

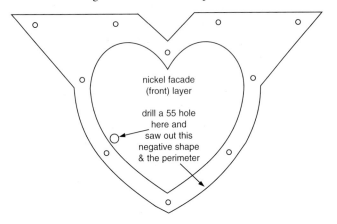

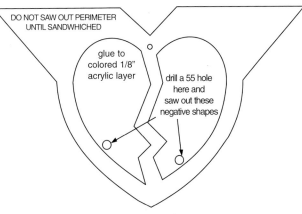

1. Gather the materials. You will eventually be making a "sandwich" of five layers stacked in the following order from top to bottom: nickel silver sheet, clear acrylic sheet, red acrylic sheet, paper image, and patterned brass sheet. Photocopy the templates at left and roughly cut them out. Use rubber cement to glue one template to the nickel silver sheet and the other template to the red acrylic sheet, as labeled (below).

2. The nickel silver sheet is the façade, or front layer. Use a jeweler's saw to cut out the perimeter. Then, use a #55 bit to drill a hole and cut out the interior heart shape of the façade. *Do not* cut out any other layers at this time. Using the façade as a frame, choose an image or photo that fills the frame. Use a photocopier to adjust the size, if needed. Your chosen image will be the image layer that lines the back of the heart-shaped box.

3. Use a #55 bit to drill all ten holes in the façade layer (indicated by small circles on the template). Next, use the façade layer as a template to drill ten holes in each succeeding layer

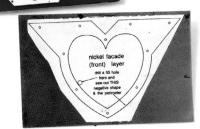

(clear acrylic sheet, red acrylic sheet, image, patterned brass sheet), one layer at a time. Before drilling the red acrylic sheet, be sure to line up the façade with the template.

4. Remove the paper template from the façade layer. Using a bench block and chasing tools, apply a decorative pattern to the surface of the façade layer, if desired.

5. Drill and cut out the two interior broken heart shapes from the red acrylic sheet (see photo below, left). Remove the paper template from the acrylic.

6. Stack and align all the layers together in order as listed in step 1. (Note that the patterned side of the brass should face out, away from the other layers.) Secure this "sandwich" together by inserting the copper rivets into the ten drilled holes and through all the layers. Flip the sandwich over to the back layer, and then use small-nose pliers to bend the copper rivets over toward the center of the sandwich.

7. Using the façade layer as a guide, cut out the perimeter through all four lower layers (below, right). File the cutout sandwich edges to blend all the layers together, and then use steel wool to bring the edges of the sandwich to a smooth finish.

8. Straighten the rivets and disassemble the sandwich. Position the pin back on the back of the brass layer

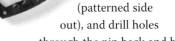

(patterned side out), and drill holes through the pin back and brass layer. Rivet the pin back to the backing layer using two copper rivets (as shown above, left). If you wish, treat the patterned façade and backing layers with patina solution, then use steel wool to bring out the pattern.

9. Using a #52 drill bit, re-drill and enlarge all the holes in all layers *except* the backing layer. Use a 0-80 tap to thread the existing holes in the backing layer.

10. Match up and stack all the layers, starting from the backing layer. When you get to the red acrylic layer, insert small mementos or found objects to be contained in the two-section box. Continue by adding the clear acrylic layer and the façade layer.

11. Insert a 0-80 hex head bolt in each hole, threading each bolt into the tapped holes in the back layer. Leave the bolts a little loose so that you can align the layers precisely. Then, snug down (but don't tighten) all the bolts.

12. To make the piece a pendant as well as a pin, slide necklace tabs over the two outermost bolt ends at the top of the heart (as shown above, right). Cover each tab with a washer and nut. Spin a nut on all the reaming exposed bolt ends, and snug them down using a miniature nut driver. If the bolt ends are too long, use a flush cutter to trim the excess and then file them flush. Attach chain.

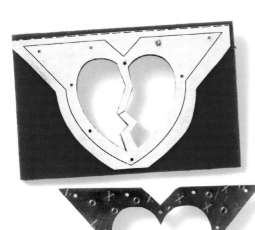

mom's personal and geographic travels necklace

Artist: **Kristin Diener**

KRISTIN DIENER'S HEARTFELT masterpiece was inspired by her mom's love of travel and sense of adventure. Kristin's one-of-a-kind labor of love incorporates many of her mother's keepsakes, including a photo of her as a young woman, an eyeglass lens, a carved bone souvenir from China, a skeletonized and plated leaf, a shell button, a gold lip shell, part of a 1979 road atlas, a handkerchief scrap, a candy wrapper, and assorted gemstones.

Materials

- Photo
- Salvaged glass, such as eyeglass or spectacle lens
- Keepsakes such as buttons, snaps, maps, stone cabochons, etc.
- Embellishments, such as precast sterling silver leaves
- Four large sterling silver jump rings
- 28-gauge fine silver bezel wire, plain and scalloped, $1/8$"/3 mm and $3/16$"/5 mm
- 28-gauge sterling silver sheet, approximately 3 x 2"/7.6 x 5 cm
- 26-gauge sterling silver sheet, approximately 8 x $4^1/2$"/20.3 x 11.4 cm
- 26-gauge sterling silver round wire
- Pearls and other beads
- Mica
- Sterling silver chain, approximately 21"/53.3 cm
- Sterling silver closure, such as a hook and eye clasp

Tools and Supplies

- Paper scissors
- Tracing or other paper
- Pencil or pen
- Ultrafine-point permanent marker
- Wire wrapping kit
- Finishing kit
- Advanced soldering kit
- Safety glasses
- Ring mandrel
- Sawing kit
- Pickle supplies:
  - Pickle pot
  - Water
  - Pickle
  - Copper tongs
  - Glass bowl (for water bath)
  - Rubber gloves
  - Apron
- Drilling kit (hand drill) with #59, $5/64$"/2 mm, and $7/64$"/2.8 mm drill bits
- Chasing tool of your choice

- Bench block
- Chasing or other hammer
- Patina kit
- Metal shears
- Bezel rocker
- Digital camera (optional)
- Photocopier or computer with imaging software, scanner, and printer (optional)

MAKE IT YOUR OWN

To make your own version, find a photo of a family member or person special to you. Gather objects that represent your loved one's personal and geographic travels through life. (Or, use an image of an unknown person and build a fictional travel story of objects around it.) Design a small piece that includes just a few keepsakes around a central photo, or go for broke and create a full-size wonder like Kristin's.

1. Select a central item or theme around which to build the necklace pendant. Kristin used a photo encased behind an eyeglass lens. If you wish, use your computer's imaging software or a photocopier to adjust the color and size of the photo as desired and print it out. Cut the image to fit behind the glass.

2. Choose keepsakes and stones that go with the original theme. Kristin chose objects reflecting who her mother is and where she traveled. Begin laying out these objects in a design, focusing on balance. If you want, include a central design motif, such as a hand shape. Kristin's designs are often asymmetrical, so instead of creating a symmetrical arrangement of pairs of matching objects,

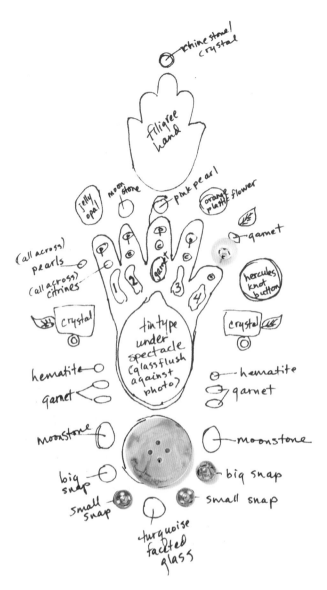

rhinestone/crystal

filigree hand

jelly opal _moonstone_ _pink pearl_ _orange plastic flower_

garnet

(all across) _pearls_ _garnet_

(all across) _citrines_

hercules knot button

crystal _crystal_

tintype under spectacle (glass flush against photo)

hematite _hematite_

garnet _garnet_

moonstone _moonstone_

big snap _big snap_

small snap _small snap_

turquoise faceted glass

chain.

4. Once objects are selected and the design is complete, make a sketch of the design, labeling individual objects (see photo, left). This record of your design will serve as a road map as you create the piece. You might also take a photograph of your proposed arrangement of objects.

5. Use bezel wire to make bezels for each object and stone (see photo below). Think of a bezel as the sidewall of a cup in which each object will sit. Wrap bezel wire around each object, mark the wire where the ends overlap, and cut the wire with a wire cutter. File the ends and fit them together. Flux the ends and use hard solder and a torch to solder each bezel shut. Once soldered, use pliers (such as needle- or chain-nose) to shape, or mold, each bezel to the object or stone. The fit should be tight, but loose enough so the object can still be dropped into the bezel from above. For round cabochon bezels, Kristin places the bezels on a ring mandrel and molds them with her fingers.

Be Careful: When soldering, work in a well-ventilated area and use care when working with the flame. Pull back and secure long hair. Wear safety glasses and keep a fire extinguisher nearby.

6. On 28-gauge sterling silver sheet, sketch a hand shape (or other central motif), and cut it out with a jeweler's saw. Use files and steel wool to finish the edges. Turn the hand over, flux the entire back of the hand, and melt medium solder onto the back. Cut a large rectangular piece of 26-gauge sterling silver sheet, which will become the base of the pendant. Flux the entire rectangular piece. Turn the hand over again and place it in position on the base.

she arranges similar objects so they balance "by eye" or appear to add the same visual "weight" to the piece. Consider including metal embellishments—such as precast stampings and jump rings—for added dimension.

Tip: Kristin suggests that as you design and fabricate a piece, be flexible and open to new ideas that come to you. Allow them to influence and change the design as you progress. A fluid design can result in a more interesting final product.

3. As you consider how your piece will work aesthetically, plan how it will function as jewelry. Ask yourself questions such as: Where will the pendant meet the chain? How will the chain be attached to the pendant? Kristin's pendant has two holes drilled on either side of the "shoulder" through which jump rings pass and attach the pendant to the

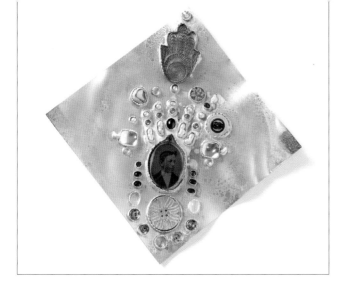

7. Flux the top surface of the hand. Flux all the bezels and place them in position according to your design sketch. At this point, Kristin also fluxes and positions any embellishments, such as the precast leaves and jump rings. Then she uses medium solder and a torch to solder all the pieces, including the hand, bezels, and embellishments, to the base at one time.

8. Let the piece cool slightly, and then place it in pickle until clean. Pickle is an acidic solution (such as water and sodium bisulphate) used to remove oxidation and flux from the surface of metal. In a pickle pot, Kristin mixes and heats a solution of water and sodium bisulphate and places the metal piece in it. Once it is clean, remove the piece and rinse it in a bowl of water. Check the solder joints to make sure they are still completely soldered. Repair any incomplete joints using easy solder and a torch, then once again clean the piece in pickle and rinse it.

Be Careful: When using pickle, follow the manufacturer's instructions. Work in a well-ventilated area. Wear gloves, an apron, and safety glasses.

9. When all soldering is completed, Kristin suggests that you check your design by temporarily placing the objects and stones in the bezels (as shown above), taking care not to get them stuck. If she is not pleased with the design, Kristin makes any needed changes at this point, adding (using easy solder) or removing design elements.

10. Carefully remove any objects and stones you temporarily placed in the bezels. Use an ultrafine-point marker to begin drawing where you intend to saw. This includes the outer edge of the pendant, cutouts between fingers and stones, holes inside jump rings, and cutouts within bezels (which will serve as "windows" when

viewed from the back of the necklace, as shown at right). Use a jeweler's saw to cut out the outer edge of the pendant. Then use a hand drill with a #59 drill bit to pierce the cutouts and saw them out.

11. Drill two holes at the shoulder of the pendant using a $^7/_{64}$"/2.8 mm drill bit. Use a $^5/_{64}$"/2 mm bit to drill holes from which to hang beads. File and finish the pendant with steel wool. Use a chasing tool of your choice and a bench block to chase a pattern all around the outer edge.

12. Use liver of sulfur or another patina solution (following the instructions on page 22) to give the pendant, jump rings, wire, and chain an aged appearance. Polish the metal pieces using the method of your choice (see page 23).

13. Cut lengths of 26-gauge sterling silver round wire to make head pins for hanging beads. Use round-nose pliers to make a small loop at one end of each wire. String beads and pearls on the wire as desired. Use wire wrapping (following the instructions on page 21) to hang the beads from the holes drilled in the pendant.

14. Prepare the bezels for setting. To raise all the objects within the bezels to the desired height, insert below them as many sheets of mica (cut to size with shears or scissors) as needed. For any paper or fabric keepsake (maps, candy wrappers, handkerchief) you want visible from the bottom of the piece, sandwich it between sheets of mica, cut the sandwich to size, and place the sandwich in the bottom of the bezel. Then, place a stone or other object (carved bone, leaf, etc.) on top of the sandwich. (Kristin's central design element consists of, from bottom to top, mica, a map, mica, a photo, a cut candy wrapper, and an eyeglass lens.) Insert all the objects and set all the bezels using a bezel rocker.

15. Cut two pieces of purchased chain (or use handmade chain, as Kristin used) to the desired length. Use two jump rings to attach the chain to the pendant. Attach a closure to the chain.

leaving home necklace

Artist: **Kristin Diener**

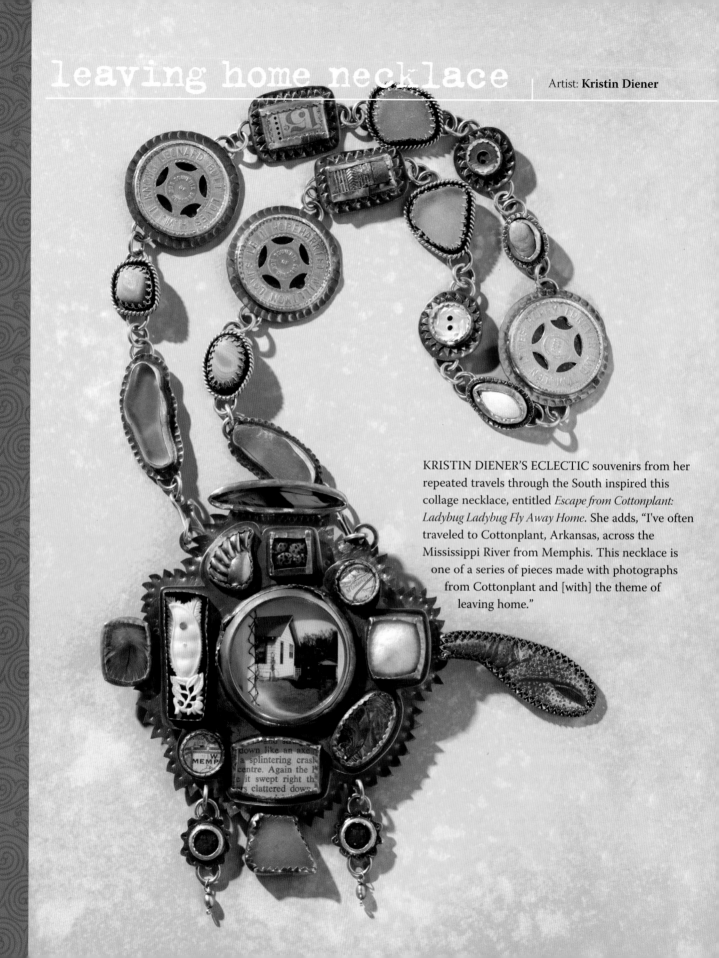

KRISTIN DIENER'S ECLECTIC souvenirs from her repeated travels through the South inspired this collage necklace, entitled *Escape from Cottonplant: Ladybug Ladybug Fly Away Home*. She adds, "I've often traveled to Cottonplant, Arkansas, across the Mississippi River from Memphis. This necklace is one of a series of pieces made with photographs from Cottonplant and [with] the theme of leaving home."

Materials

- Photo
- Souvenirs and found objects such as maps, text, feathers, coins, etc.
- Salvaged glass and plastic, such as watch crystals
- 28-gauge fine silver bezel wire, plain and scalloped, ⅛"/3 mm and ³⁄₁₆"/5 mm
- 26-gauge fine silver sheet
- 26-gauge sterling silver sheet, approximately 8 x 8"/20.3 x 20.3 cm
- 26-gauge red brass sheet, approximately 8 x 8"/20.3 x 20.3 cm
- ⅛"/3 mm plexiglass sheet

- 10-gauge sterling silver round wire
- Pearl and other beads
- Mica
- Large sterling silver jump rings
- 26-gauge copper sheet
- 26-gauge yellow brass sheet
- 18-gauge sterling silver twisted or square wire
- Two sterling silver hook closures
- 26-gauge sterling silver round wire (optional)

Tools and Supplies

- All tools and supplies used for the Mom's Personal and Geographic Travels Necklace project (see page 131)
- #38 drill bit
- Riveting kit
- Balsa wood (optional)

MAKE IT YOUR OWN

To make your own version, think about a road trip you took, a favorite vacation, or what "leaving home" means to you. Gather souvenirs from your past travels, or collect them during your next trip.

1. Decide on a central theme or story for your necklace. Choose a central photo and related objects based upon your theme. Don't discount unusual things like soil and cotton. Add or subtract objects to create your design. Plan how you will encase fragile items behind glass or plastic, such as watch crystals. Consider how the piece will function as a necklace. Note that Kristin's design consists of a pendant made from a grouping of bezel-set objects and several individual bezel-set objects that form the links of the necklace chain. You may also wish to include some objects that hang or protrude from the pendant, like Kristin's plastic lobster claw, beach glass, and green feathers. If you wish, take a photo of your design.

2. Follow step 5 on page 132 to make, solder, and shape a bezel for each object. For objects that are too tall for conventional bezel wire, Kristen cuts bezel strips from 26-gauge fine silver sheet. After they are soldered, be sure to perfectly shape each bezel to the object so the object can easily be dropped into the bezel from above (see photo page 136, top). Set aside the objects and bezels that will be links in the necklace chain until you reach step 15.

shears any excess metal on the base of each bezel cup, and file as needed.

7. Place the silver pendant piece onto a piece of 26-gauge red brass sheet, which will become another layer of the base of the pendant. Position and mark on the red brass where you will attach the bezel cups for the protruding objects and the two jumps rings for attaching the chain to pendant. Sketch the perimeter shape you want as well as the circular cutout "window" in the red brass piece to reveal the star-shaped cutout in the silver piece. Set aside the silver pendant piece, and then saw out and file the red brass.

8. Repeat steps 3 and 4 to solder (using medium solder) the protruding bezel cups and jump rings (using easy solder) onto the red brass sheet, and to clean the piece, check it, and repair it (if needed).

9. Use liver of sulfur or another patina solution (following the instructions on page 22) to give the silver pendant piece an aged appearance. Polish the piece using the method of your choice (see page 23).

10. Use a chasing tool of your choice to chase a pattern all around the outer edge of the red brass pendant piece. Use sandpaper and a steel wire brush to give it a matte finish.

11. The silver pendant piece eventually will be riveted to the red brass pendant piece with a layer of plexiglass sandwiched in between. At this time, mark the position of future rivet holes on the silver pendant piece inside some of the bezel cups (which will help hide the rivets when viewed from above).

3. To assemble the pendant, first cut a large circular piece of 26-gauge sterling silver sheet, which will become one layer of the base of the pendant. Flux the entire piece. Flux all the bezels (except those of the protruding objects), and place them in position according to your design. Use medium solder and a torch to solder all the bezels to the base at one time.

4. Follow step 8 on page 133 to clean, check, and repair the silver pendant piece.

5. Use an ultrafine-point marker to begin drawing where you intend to saw, including the outer edge of the silver pendant piece and a star-shaped cutout "window" within the central photo bezel (see photo page 137, top). Use a jeweler's saw to cut out the outer edge of the pendant. Then use a #59 drill bit and hand drill to pierce the cutout and saw it out. File the edges.

6. Make an individual bezel cup for each of the protruding objects by fluxing and soldering (using medium solder) the bezels to fluxed pieces of 26-gauge red brass or sterling silver sheet. Saw or cut out with

three layers. Use 10-gauge sterling silver wire to make rivets (following the instructions on page 19), and set them in each hole. Next, follow step 14 on page 133 to raise the remaining pendant objects and set the bezels with rivets in them.

14. Use a ⁵⁄₆₄"/2 mm bit to drill holes from which to hang objects from the pendant. Use jump rings to attach found objects or embellishments from the holes. Or, follow the instructions on page 54 to make head pins, and use wire wrapping to hang beads from the pendant.

15. Get the objects and bezels for the necklace chain that you set aside in step 2. Make an individual bezel cup for each object by fluxing and soldering (using medium solder) the bezels to fluxed pieces of 26-gauge copper, yellow brass, or sterling silver sheet (see photo page 136, bottom). Vary their appearance by soldering on lengths of 18-gauge twisted or square wire to some bezel cups and chasing patterns on others (after sawing them out), or by soldering silver bezel cups onto yellow brass or copper sheet. Saw or cut out with shears any excess metal on the base of each bezel cup to the desired shape, and then clean and file the bezel cups.

16. Solder (using easy solder) two jump rings on the back of each bezel cup. Follow step 8 on page 133 to clean, check, and repair (if needed) the bezel cups and jump rings. Treat the bezel cups with patina solution and polish them. Raise all the objects within the bezels to the desired height and set them. Attach jump rings to link the bezel cups together to form a chain. Attach a silver hook at either end of the chain, and use the hooks to attach the chain to the pendant.

12. Follow step 14 on page 133 to prepare and set the pendant bezels (including the protruding objects) using a bezel rocker. Use mica to raise all the objects within the bezels to the desired height and set them, but *do not* set those bezel cups within which rivets will be placed.

Tip: When you have unusually shaped objects, it may be hard to raise them up enough using only thin mica. In such cases, Kristin cuts to size pieces of thicker balsa wood or plexiglass and uses them to raise the objects.

13. Use a saw to cut a piece of plexiglass just a little smaller than the silver pendant piece, and sandwich it between the silver and brass pendant pieces. Using a #38 bit, drill the rivet holes (where previously marked) through all

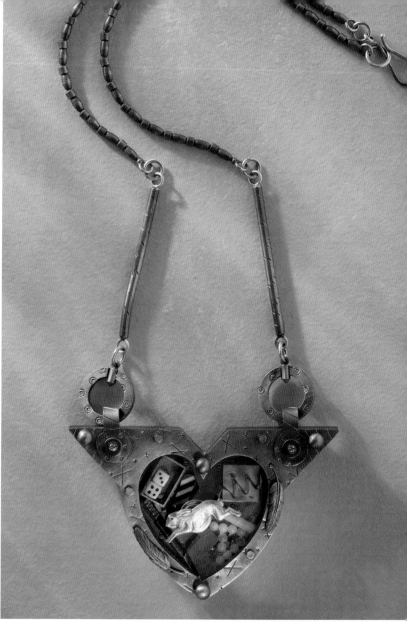

Marlene True
(above)

Prince Albert, Out of the Can, 2005, 2½ x 1³/₄ x ⅛"/6.4 x 4.4 x .3 cm. Sterling silver, copper, tin, 18K gold, diamond.

"When looking at my collection of Prince Albert tins, I was reminded of the childhood question or joke, 'Do you have Prince Albert in a can?' I decided to let the guy out and give him a fancy new lapel pin. I like the idea of my jewelry wearing jewelry."

Thomas Mann
(above)

This Heart Box Necklace, 1990, 2¼ x 3½"/5.6 x 8.9 cm. Brass, bronze, acrylic, dice.

"I was looking at a medical diagram of the heart one day when it occurred to me that the 'chambers' of the heart could also be 'containers,' which in fact they are. Containers for the fluid of life, so why not extend that meaning to the flow of objects we experience in our lives and make a container for those things that are the most important to us?"

Thomas Mann
(above)

Girl with Fish Pin, 1988,
5 x 2½"/12.7 x 6.4 cm.
Sterling silver, brass,
acrylic, antique photo,
micarta, aluminum.

"Combing through a flea
market in Paris, I found
a number of antique photos
of women holding 'bouquets'
of fish, which the
vendor told me were
April Fools cards. People
used to actually send
fish as April Fools
jokes, but this practice
had evolved into sending
'fish' postcards as a
nod to the historic
joke. This was just too
good, so it had to
become a series, and I
had to buy a lot of
these cards."

Thomas Mann
(above)

Mokume Photo Pin, 1989,
2¾ x 2¼"/6.9 x 5.6 cm.
Sterling silver, copper,
mokume, acrylic,
antique photo.

"[This is made with] a
material called mokume... a
Japanese metalsmithing
technique in which you
laminate layers of copper
and silver together and
adhere them with heat and
pressure, then carve and
sand through the layers in
different ways to create
patterns, which can
resemble wood grain.
Traditionally it was used
on the hilts and hand
guards on Samurai swords."

Kristin Diener
(above)

Red Lady, 1997, 5½ x 2 ½ x ¼"/14 x 6.4 x .6 cm (13"/33 cm long with chain).

Sterling silver, fine silver, eyeglass frame, portrait with glass cover, brooch, shell buttons, beach glass, pearls, carnelian, shell bird, stone, glass bead.

"The portrait of the woman is one I found a long time ago in an Ohio thrift store. I combined her with beach glass from Rhode Island, Aunt Verna's silver brooch, shell buttons from Boston, and assorted other 'precious' items. This piece I held on to and wear frequently, as it reminds me of particular trips and particular locations."

Kristin Diener
(above)

Sea Horse/New Orleans Love Letter, 2005, 6½ x 4¾ x ½"/16.5 x 12.1 x 1.3 cm (18"/45.7 cm long with chain).

Sterling silver, fine silver, gold, brass, eyeglass frame and lens, goat fur, shell buttons, rutilated quartz, glass cabochon, shells, mica, candy wrapper, found objects.

"This piece was created just before Hurricane Katrina as a love letter to New Orleans."

Kristin Diener
(above)

Memento Mori, 2006, 6 x 3½ x ¼"/15.2 x 8.9 x .6 cm (13"/33 cm long with chain).

Sterling silver, fine silver, gold, eyeglass frame and lens, 1887 print, shell buttons, found objects, mica, metal foil.

"This piece is meant to commemorate the death of the boy in the 1887 print."

About the Artists -
Project Artists

Kristin Diener

Kristin Diener received her MFA in Jewelry/Metals from Bowling Green State University (Ohio), and her BA in Art, Women, and American Culture from University of Alabama (Tuscaloosa). She took her first Jewelry course from Judy Wenig-Horswell at Goshen College (Indiana) in 1980 and was immediately hooked on the materials, traditions, techniques, tools, creative possibilities, and relationship to the body of jewelry/metals. She incorporates found objects and mixed media with the precious metal and stones, to best carry out her relationship with and response to the world. (bigthumbgirl@yahoo.com)

Phoenix Forrester

Phoenix's love of jewelry began in childhood. She dreamed of being a silversmith, and in 1995 moved to New Mexico and began her apprenticeship with David Troutman. She has been making found object jewelry ever since and sells in shows and galleries across the country. Currently she teaches silversmith classes from her home studio and enjoys creating custom work for her loyal clients. (www.phoenixforrester.com)

Amy Hanna

Amy Hanna was raised in Michigan and spent a great deal of time traveling and living across America. She is now the mother of three and resides in Southern California. Amy spends her early hours of the weekends at local flea markets unleashing her creativity and finding lost treasures. Harboring a love of unique art but unable to find jewelry that represented her personal style, she began creating one-of-a-kind pieces of jewelry made from discarded treasures. Along with flea marketing, some of Amy's favorite things to do include taking art classes, teaching classes, traveling, spending time with her family, and working in her art studio. Amy has been seen on *That's Clever*, taught at Artfest, and has been featured in *Belle Armoire* magazine. (www.amyhanna.etsy.com)

Thomas Mann

Thomas Mann has been an active participant in the contemporary American craft movement for the past thirty years as an artist, gallery owner, and lecturer. He describes himself as an artist working in the medium of jewelry and sculpture. The primary design vocabulary that he employs in the making of jewelry objects combines industrial aesthetics and materials with evocative romantic themes and imagery. He calls this design system Techno Romantic. Though it is not the only design mode in which he works, it is the one for which he is best known. Thomas Mann lives and works in New Orleans, where he oversees a jewelry design and production studio, a sculpture studio, and gallery. He currently exhibits his jewelry and sculpture with some 250 galleries in the U.S. and abroad, and at premier art events around the U.S. (www.thomasmann.com)

Linda O'Brien

Linda O'Brien started out as an art major but earned her degree in Naturopathy, a practice that uses herbs and other natural remedies to promote a state of well-being. She is a self-taught artist, jewelry designer, published poet, and life student of the Metaphysical Sciences. Much of her work honors the Goddess, who in her numerous manifestations has danced at the very heart of the great traditions and is the embodiment of female strength and wisdom. (www.burntofferings.com)

Bryan Petersen

Bryan Petersen received his BA from Montana State University and his MFA from East Carolina University. He is currently an Assistant Professor of Art at Georgia Southern University. His jewelry was featured in *Fabulous Jewelry from Found Objects* (Lark Books).

Beth Piver

Beth Piver designs and creates a wide range of contemporary, mixed media jewelry. Growing up as an Air Force brat, she has lived and traveled all over the country and parts of Asia. Her formal training in graphic design, computer graphics, and photography manifests itself throughout her work in bold shapes, striking juxtapositions, and varied textures. Often oversized and exaggerated (yet wearable), each piece is constructed of silver, copper, brass, bronze, and steel and then adorned with obscure findings, spinning and moving parts, serpentine wires, paint and patinas, and computer-generated imagery. Her work is available in galleries throughout the United States, and on her Web site. (www.bethpiver.com)

Stephanie Jones Rubiano

Stephanie Jones Rubiano earned a bachelors of science degree in marine biology and worked as an environmental scientist for five years in Houston, TX, for a major oil company. So, it stands to reason that she is now an almost full-time artist who revels in the creative process. Her work has been seen on the outside and inside of such publications as *Somerset Studio, Belle Armoire, Bead and Button, The Art of Polymer Clay Jewelry, The Adventurous Scrapbooker*, and various booklets by Design Originals. She has taught classes and been a vendor at national art gatherings for the last five years, and her work has been carried in galleries and boutiques across the United States. She lives and creates in Austin, TX, with her three-year-old daughter, two cats, and assorted marine fish and invertebrates. (www.stephanierubiano.com)

Janette Schuster

Janette Schuster is a freelance writer, artist, workshop instructor, and incurable treasure hunter. Formally trained as a geologist and archaeologist, she has been digging up artifacts all her life. She now indulges her love of found relics, modern to ancient, by using them in jewelry, collage, assemblage, and mosaics. Her work has appeared in many publications, including *Somerset Studio, Cloth Paper Scissors, The Studio Zine, ARTitude Zine, Somerset Studio Gallery*, and *Return to Asia*. She lives and creates in rural New Hampshire. (www.VisualApothecary.com)

Jan Bode Smiley

A self-taught artist living in Fort Mill, SC, Jan Bode Smiley began her artistic endeavors as a quilt maker. Building on these skills, she began exploring mixed media materials and techniques. She is the author of four books on topics ranging from quilt making to travel journals. She travels internationally to teach and lecture on the subject of quilt making, fiber arts, and mixed media. (www.jansmiley.com)

Marlene True

Marlene True is a studio artist living in Greenville, NC, and currently completing her MFA at East Carolina University. She earned her BFA with a concentration in metalsmithing at Southern Illinois University, Edwardsville. Her work has been widely exhibited, with recent work focusing on narrative and color. She is represented by many galleries throughout the U.S., and her work has appeared in several books and publications, including *Fabulous Jewelry from Found Objects*, *The Fine Art of the Tin Can* (both by Lark Books), and *Art Jewelry Magazine*. She has taught metalwork workshops such as "Tin is in and Good as Gold" and "Mokume Gane" at Arrowmont School of Arts and Crafts, Made in Metal Gallery, Craft Alliance, and other art schools. (www.marlenetrue.com)

Luann Udell

Luann Udell is a nationally exhibited artist whose work is sold in fine galleries across the country. Her fiber wall hangings, polymer sculptures, and jewelry are inspired by ancient cave art and tribal art from around the world. She blogs regularly about the business of art and her life as an artist. Her book, *The Weekend Crafter: Rubber Stamp Carving*, was published by Lark Books in 2003. (www.luannudell.com)

About the Artists - Gallery Artists

Giuseppina Cirincione

Giuseppina "Josie" Cirincione does not have a degree in art, but she always found herself drawn to art and different art forms. She has taken a variety of classes based upon her interests. What started out as making simple cards for herself later led to collage art and working with different media. This opened the door for her first book, *Collage Lost and Found*. She currently teaches classes, sells her jewelry and other handmade objects at specialty boutiques, and is working on a new book, due to be published in spring 2008. (www.inkyblackpaperarts.com)

Keith Lo Bue

Keith Lo Bue is a found-object jeweler, sculptor, and teacher who has work in many major collections, including the Smithsonian Institution in Washington, DC, and the Museum of Arts and Design in New York. His work has been exhibited all around the U.S. and in Germany, Australia, New Zealand, France, Ireland, and England. Keith lives and works in Sydney, Australia. (www.lobue-art.com)

Lou McCulloch

As a former senior designer for a magazine, Lou McCulloch tries to keep up on the latest art trends. Vintage ephemera is almost always used in her mixed media, due to a lifelong interest in the subject. Lou is the author of a book about paper Americana and a reference work for photography collectors. A few years back, she became interested in combining found objects and antique photographs with this ephemera, which has become her major center of interest. Some of her work can be seen in the books *Altered Objects* and *Kaleidoscope*, and it has also been showcased in magazines such as *Somerset Gallery*, *Somerset Memories*, *Bound and Lettered*, the online magazines *Holograph* (Seattle) and *Art-e-zine*, *Artitude*, *Altered Arts*, and *Cloth, Paper, Scissors*. Currently, she builds assemblages with her talented husband. (www.alteredlou.blogspot.com)

Opie O'Brien

Opie O'Brien is both a mixed-media artist and a musician. He was a fine arts major at the School of Visual Arts in New York City, prior to that attended art classes at Pratt Institute. He is known for his fine-line and detailed style, but, being a Gemini, he can also be very whimsical. (www.burntofferings.com)

Susan Skinner

Susan Skinner is a self-taught jeweler who creates work that is influenced by her degree in anthropology. The use of an object removed from its original context has been an ongoing theme in her work. As an avid gleaner at flea markets and yard sales, she has amassed a great deal of found object materials—including rulers, buttons, postcards, lithographed tin cans, and gaming tokens—that she often uses in her jewelry. She tries to follow a less traditional form of jewelry making, giving additional life as ornamentation to items typically discarded after their intended usage. In her work, she attempts to reflect the values of simplicity in style and technique, respect for materials, and a search for harmony in one's work rather than for perfection. (www.mariposa-gallery.com)

Karen Strauss

Karen Strauss is a mixed media artist living in the Bahamas. Her challenge is dividing her time between her metal clay work, jewelry making, digital imaging, and travel. Her muse is the ocean that she gazes upon from her studio window. She has a background in magazine publishing and has raised four children; the oldest is Helga Strauss, owner of ARTchix Studio. (www.artchixstudio.com)

Alison Woodward

After studying Interior Design and Architectural Preservation, Alison Woodward began to design jewelry using antique and vintage materials. Inspired by all things historic, she designs every piece in such a way as to highlight each element's most exquisite or unusual detail, resulting in a beautifully proportioned and intricately constructed piece of jewelry. Designed by Alison Woodward, Reverie is a line of one-of-a-kind jewelry that launched out of New York City in 2003. (www.reverienyc.com)

Acknowledgments

I would like to thank the artists who generously donated their time and talent to this project, particularly Stephanie Jones Rubiano and Kristin Diener who went beyond the call of duty. Thanks also go to my family and friends for their love, support, and encouragement. I owe a huge debt of gratitude to those artists who have and continue to inspire and teach me, including Keith Lo Bue, Thomas Mann, and Keely Barham.

Notes on Suppliers

Usually, the supplies you need for making the projects in Lark books can be found at your local craft supply store, discount mart, home improvement center, or retail shop relevant to the topic of the book. Occasionally, however, you may need to buy materials or tools from specialty suppliers. In order to provide you with the most up-to-date information, we have created a listing of suppliers on our Web site, which we update on a regular basis. Visit us at www.larkbooks.com, click on "Craft Supply Sources," and then click on the relevant topic. You will find numerous companies listed with their Web address and/or mailing address and phone number.

Index